Legal Services and Digital Infrastructures

This book seeks to provide a better understanding and to promote a more responsive and inclusive governance of the automation and digital devices in public institutions, particularly the law and justice sector.

Concerns related to artificial intelligence (herein AI) design and use have been exacerbated recently with the recognition of the discriminatory potential that can be embedded into AI applications in public service institutions. This book also examines some critical issues relating to the assigning of responsibility in a public service produced and delivered on the basis of an automated mechanism. Above all, the analysis and vision offered in the book encourage critical thinking about the legal services and the justice institutions as they are transformed by AI and automation. This vision aims to raise awareness as to the prospect of transformation we face in terms of responsibility and of agency and the need to design a citizen-centred and human rights-compliant system of technology assessment and AI monitoring and evaluation. The book calls for a comprehensive strategy to enable professional practitioners and decision-makers to engage in the design of AI-driven legal and justice services, but it points out the shortcoming perspective that is entrenched into the idea of quality by design. To make sure that the transformation undergone by legal services and justice responses in relationship to the advancements of digital technologies and the information and data sciences is fully respectful of the foundational principles of our democratic societies, the perspective offered in this book aims to add to the engagement of designers and users, in addition to the regular and rigorous contribution of the "voice" of the research. Only by mapping the effects triggered – intentionally and not intentionally – by the digital transformation and discovering the unpredictable and still possible consequences that AI and ICT may entail once they interplay "in context" with the legal procedures, the legal competences, the organizational skills and routines, and the rituals featured by the justice systems, the existence of a gap between the actual functioning of the justice systems thereby transformed and the respect of the fundamental rights of citizens are eventually assessed and promptly filled.

The work inspiring the book draws on ongoing research and consulting activities carried out by the author across different countries and different systems in the legal and justice sector.

In the following pages a new mindset among legal professionals and the justice institutions is promoted, thus empowering and training them to develop the necessary responsiveness and accountability in the justice sector and legal systems. It will also be of interest to researchers and academics working in the area of AI, Public Law, Human Rights, and Criminal Justice.

Daniela Piana is Professor of Political Science at the University of Bologna, Italy, Associate Researcher at the ENS Université Paris Saclay, member of the OECD Advisory Group on Justice, and member of the Scientific Committee at the Italian Administrative Supreme Court.

Legal Services and Digital Infrastructures

A New Compass for Better Governance

Daniela Piana

LONDON AND NEW YORK

First published 2021
by Routledge
2 Park Square, Milton Park, Abingdon, Oxon OX14 4RN

and by Routledge
52 Vanderbilt Avenue, New York, NY 10017

Routledge is an imprint of the Taylor & Francis Group, an informa business

British Library Cataloguing-in-Publication Data
A catalogue record for this book is available from the British Library

Library of Congress Cataloging-in-Publication Data
A catalog record has been requested for this book

ISBN: 978-0-367-54972-5 (hbk)
ISBN: 978-1-003-09141-7 (ebk)

Typeset in Times New Roman
by Newgen Publishing UK

To those who dare
sailing in the open seas

Contents

Foreword   ix
Acknowledgements   xi

1 **Sailing in open sea**   1
   People must gain the centre of the agenda 9

2 **Reframing the digital picture**   17
   Stories one may read 17
   Three waves of digital transformation 18
   The fourth dimension: artificial intelligence coming in 28
   The unreliability of the technological promise 34

3 **In search of fairness**   38
   A tale of ideal cities 38
   The social dimension of legality 39
   Qualities of justice people want 43
   Reasons to trust 50

4 **System of intelligences**   57
   Stories we presumably shall read 57
   The factor within the engine of a complex system 57
   Intelligible because meaningful 60
   Intelligent because organized 65
   Beyond learning: the gap artificial intelligence will not fill 68

5 **Leverages of change in the justice system**   71
   Theories that make the difference 71
   A fundamental matrix: equality as the core issue 72

Governing change with standards 76
Inspiring cases 82

**6 A new compass for legal professionals, stakeholders,
   and policy makers**   93
A dance of intelligence 93
Towards a citizen-centred standard-setting process 95
Technologies and guarantees 100
A responsive toolkit 102
Actors and strategies 107
Trustworthy legal services for all 111

Conclusion   115
A choral perspective 115
A role to play for the "knowledge-holders" 117

Index   120

Foreword

In a satiric essay recently published, "Ressusité!", Marc Augé portraits an unprecedented type of heroism, the one that a human being experiences after a long period of disconnection from the real life. An academic scholar, who died because of cancer, is subjected to cryogenic therapy and after 70 years spent at –90° is brought to life again. The lapse of time that separates 1968 (the year of death) from 2028 (the year of the rebirth) is significant enough in terms of discontinuity and novelty, in all the fields of the human and social life. In the new life he finds a way to get connected to the people he wants to reach through social media and the digital transformation in the meantime impinges upon the social interactions transfiguring and discontinuing all the ways traditionally used to share, communicate, get in touch, dissent, consent, negotiate, resist, adapt, and so on (Woolgar, 1991).

Certainly, connections can reach out all over. Space distances have become insignificant. But still something is missing. The scent, the touch, the taste are lost. The digital world is made of eyes and ears.

The satiric approach does not make any less revealing the story that the novel is telling us and offers a nice anchor for the argument that is offered in the book about the qualities of the legal services and the justice responses that the digital infrastructures make possible and, at the same time, need. If, on the one hand, the digital infrastructures may incorporate a part of the "intelligence" that is embodied into the legal and justice institutions, on the other hand some other parts of the "intelligence" of the socio-legal systems are lost. They relate mostly either to the needs experienced by people when they have problems in social and economic life or to the capacities and skills developed by people employed in justice institutions. Replacing these types of intelligence by a unique form of intelligence seems to be reductive and shortcoming. The book makes a stronger claim with regard to the model of governance that a world of legal services and justice institutions irrigated by digital devices requires: this model is based on a reflexive, responsive, and participative combination of standards – legal, technical, ethical, and social – that are taken as azimuth in the design, development, and assessment of the legal services and the justice responses that incorporate massive doses of technology.

The reader this book addresses is the one that experiences the world of the law, of courts, the law firms, as well as the practitioner and the policy maker that engages in a process of public policy, policy design and implementation, or standard-setting.

The reader will find an uncommon approach in the language and the narrative. One of the most innovative and strongest presuppositions that lie at the basis of the book is that a humanistic eye cast upon the digital transformation must take seriously the huge richness of languages, semantics, examples, and metaphors that are offered to humankind by the arts and the humanities. Therefore, alongside this idea, the chapters are headed by a case or a story that recall the extra-legal world: a way to show in practice that the legal and the formal dimensions of the justice world are rooted in a broader humus of culture, from which they must keep going, drawing on their significance and their social legitimacy.

Acknowledgements

I am indebted to all the "sailors" of the open sea that have been attending the seminars hosted within the Institut des Sciences Sociales du Politique of the École normale supérieure of Paris-Saclay. This includes, with particular emphasis, the young scholars and researchers I have had the chance to meet there, whose comments, insights, remarks, and research are of utmost inspiration to all of us. A warm acknowledgement is addressed to the people with whom I have had the privilege to collaborate with within UNESCO and OECD, and with whom I share the pleasure of curiosity, creativity, and civic engagement: among them, I feel especially grateful to Lydia Ruprecht and Tatiana Teplova. I have developed the ideas that stand at the core of this book across a rich range of research working sites, which cover the fieldwork made within the Italian Ministry of Justice. Again, as in many contexts, actors make the difference and I found in Barbara Fabbrini and Alessandra Cataldi two extraordinary models combining vision and care for the "devil is in the detail". Last, I value as of incommensurable richness the experience of sharing the research and the intellectual journey with Stephanie Lacour: the encounter between a lawyer who can see beyond the disciplinary walls and who dares to step beyond them, and a social scientist who has a strong inclination for arts and all the intelligences that do not express themselves through formal and rational languages. I am also deeply grateful to Claire Bell for the outstanding work on the manuscript. This book is dedicated to all people that dare to sail across the open sea ... and do it mostly in silence.

1 Sailing in open sea

Time will tell whether we are engaging with the right method, on the right agenda. We know one common goal that we must have on the agenda: that is, ensuring that each legal need finds the appropriate path to receive, in the end, a fair, reliable, intelligible, and responsive response.

Having this goal in mind and fully acknowledging the disruptive potential of the digital transformation, one thing we may safely state: today is the right time to engage in a cooperative pattern of institutional design and public awareness enhancement to develop a new compass to govern the digital infrastructures that irrigate "justice systems".[1]

Three valuable principles must inspire this compass: pluralism, trustworthiness, and empirical responsiveness.

Two compelling reasons encourage advancing in the direction of building together a common compass having, as an inspiring principle, the ideal of a fair justice to all: the words "crisis" and "humanism" express synthetically both these reasons.

The concept of "crisis" under discussion is the one rooted in classical culture. In classical times, this concept referred to a critical juncture calling for a crucial and irreversible decision. Referring to the classical philosophy and, even more interestingly, to the classical understandings of the word, the revisited notion of crisis seems to gain an enlightening meaning with Reinhart Koselleck: the "krisis" is mirrored in a sliding door mechanism, such as the one a legal act entails ("urteilsfindung") (Koselleck 1972). Revisiting the notion of "crisis" through a historical anchoring is particularly necessary for our contemporary society, which is facing a combination of two crises, one that hits the connection between laypeople and the law and the other that influences the relationship between justice systems and technological advancements.

---

1 The semantic of the concept of "justice system" is clarified in this chapter in the next section.

Expressing these terms means reframing the "krisis" in terms of a transformative critical juncture.[2]

This requires revisiting the pathways through which social needs and values attune to the law and justice institutions, and vice versa. This act, which consists of reviewing our categories, looks very promising from the perspective of going beyond a narrow and somewhat partial view that we have long taken for granted. The reader will be offered a wide range of examples where we highlight the importance of the semantics that we more or less explicitly endorse when we use the key concepts of the mainstreaming narrative about the digital dimension of the rule of law and the justice institution. In many different contexts, the critical review of the words used in the international debate looks very useful in order to take a more aware stance towards the implicit premises these words lead us to accept. One example of this refers to the use of quality of justice. As this book tries to prove, a people-centred perspective leads us to achieve a more responsive, a more fair, and consequently a more acceptable approach to the quality of justice. In the proposal the book puts forth the dimensions of performance and of efficiency, as well as the dimension of formal correctness, all deemed parts – important parts – of a broader perspective.

To assess the appropriateness of the justice response, the book makes a clear claim: the starting point must be the assessment of the legal needs that the society experiences.

The concept of an "appropriate answer" would be equally partially conceived if it were reduced to the pure effective/efficient dimension. What else is necessary to create a genuinely "appropriate answer"? In which manner and under which conditions could digital infrastructures be instrumental in ensuring that appropriateness?

The link between the responsiveness and the governance of the digital infrastructures' design, development, and use is reassessed in Chapter 6 and in the Conclusion of this book. Here it may be helpful to seriously consider what a few scholars from different perspectives have said:

> if the law is understood to be an internal feature of social situations, rather simply an autonomous force acting upon them, we also need

---

2 In the fields of social and political science a critical juncture is meant to denote a turning point in the process of change, where several factors are playing as concomitant causes of change. More precisely, critical junctures are recalled in historical institutionalism with reference to the intervention of punctual social facts that endanger a cluster of consequences impinging disruptively upon the state of a matter (Capoccia 2015).

to understand how and in what ways these very same situations are constructed by something we call law.

(Ewick and Silbey 1998, p. 35)

Or from another perspective: "what we aim is grasping the social processes that unfold within the production and the evolution of the law" (Commaille 1994). This remark points to the substratum of the legal and institutional phenomena that is embedded in the tacit dimension of knowledge (Polanyi 1966), which is, however, not directly addressed in this book.

"Justice systems" are the most promising and heuristically powerful level of analysis at which to gain a deep and wide understanding of the interaction between people and the law. A justice system is

> here a complex interlace of structures, functions, formal and informal rules comprising the whole interface between demands and offers of justice, procedures, routines, practices, embedded know how, and institutionalized problem solving patterns that are adopted, developed, adapted, interpreted, and muddled by situated actors, i.e. lawyers, legal consultants, clerks, judges and prosecutors, experts of mediation, legal officers, attorneys.
>
> (Piana 2016)

Reference to the "justice system" means distancing oneself from two inadequate assumptions that are today prevalent in the international debate: a) justice as a law-centred sector; b) justice as a court-centred system. Both these assumptions are inadequate in probing the nature of the relationship that links society to justice.[3]

The socio-legal scholarship offers a vast range of examples. Let's mention one case as a way of instanciating the general reasoning we want to develop (see for a broader analysis Lacour and Commaille 2019). Let's take, for example, the case of two landowners who escalate a long-standing tension regarding the border between their own tenants. Even before being confronted by a legal dilemma they experience a

---

3 Both these assumptions originate from an overestimated assessment of the homogeneity featured by the legal needs expressed or experienced by citizens. The "demand" of justice, in a way, is made by a vast variety of different phenomenological situations and experiences where the notion of justice must be appraised in sociolegal terms – rather than in purely legal and formalistic terms. To achieve a better understanding of it, we must respond to the question: "What is asking for a citizen that demands a response from the justice institutions?" The answer is empirical and deserves an empirical treatment.

practical problem: who has the right to access the small river to water the crops. They may both go to see a lawyer, or, depending on the domestic legal context, they may opt for an extra-judicial settlement. They may ultimately go for a more risky but less costly solution: they try to reach a private agreement, which may over time become embedded into the customary law. This is one of the many faces of the justice system as a complex phenomenon.

Similarly, the shift to remote management of hearings and the consequent adjustment of the pattern of interactions that lawyers undertake with, on the one hand, the clerk office and, on the other hand, the defendant, are faces of the justice system. A justice system is therefore made up not only by formal normativity, but also by social normativity (Commaille 2015).

This notion provides an analytical window to cast fresh light upon the encounter between justice and digital technology. From this angle, technology appears as a macro phenomenon – emerging and manifesting itself through a vast and comprehensive phenomenology – of a socio-technical nature: despite being irrigated by technological artifacts, societies, and social facts still keep functioning on the basis of an intrinsically "social" mechanism: reflexivity. It is because we mean to create a recognizable value that we use remote conferencing: maybe to reduce travel costs, maybe to ensure easy access for all and especially those who are less advantaged, maybe to enable recording and archiving. Similarly, computational tools are applied to a massive dataset to draw information and model public services – among which legal services provided to citizens and society – with an expected higher sustainability. And yet, technology does not play simply the role of an enabler. It reshuffles the mechanisms of social coordination, transforms the agency-structure interfaces, and redesigns the boundaries between spaces and functions (Avgerou and Madon 2004). Accordingly, the encounter between justice and digital technology must be observed, assessed, and ultimately governed through the lens and the tools that are most appropriate for social facts (Forum 2018).

By focusing on the encounter between justice systems and digital technology one avoids both an apocalyptic stance and an undiscerning position towards the scenarios opened by new digital tools and technological achievements in the field of legal services and justice institutions (which are crucial building blocks of the justice system).

The concept of humanism therefore comes as a second, strong reason to engage with the intellectual and practical trajectory this book investigates. We have for a long time been trading off principles in return for short-term and over-simplified solutions (De Monticelli 2015). Roberta De Monticelli expresses this point in terms of abdication from values to facts. In a more policy-oriented perspective, the "factual dominance" entails that the regularities detected in the overall patterns of behaviours are assumed as normative criteria. In many respects, the development of standards that are driven by diffuse effective and efficient practices run the risk of falling victim to this trap, which scholars qualify as the concept of "naturalistic fallacy". As will be discussed in Chapter 5, data-driven patterns are taken as normative criteria to lead and shape future behaviours. When case law analytics provides normative parameters to orient the decision of a justice actor, we observe the shift from factual knowledge to normative reasoning. However, this shift must be treated with extreme caution. A further example of normative implications triggered by digital transformation is the one experienced in the interplay between human actors and automated devices. Technology introduces countless sources of micro-obligations and micro-constraints in the deployment of our behaviours. Therefore, this book tries to seriously reconsider, in the field of legal services production and distribution, the issue of "normativity" with a careful eye cast on the role played by the digital sources of normativity.

The simple use of the term "intelligence", in the expression "artificial intelligence" (AI), is normative.

At the basis of the arguments deployed in this book there is a pluralistic understanding of the socio-legal phenomena which goes hand to hand with a pluralistic understanding of the socio-technological phenomena. Legal norms and technical standards intervene in the social matrix, within social behaviours and at the interface between social patterns of interactions. The combination of socio-legal facts and socio-technological facts gives rise to a complex system: it would be a way to mislead and oversimplify if one assumes that the relationship that exists between, on the one hand, law and society and, on the other hand, between law and technology, or between society and technology, is linear and subjected to a reductionist rationale. Three different genera of normativity coexist: social, legal, and technological. This is the fascinating and the challenging nature of the legal and justice services that we are observing at the aube of the 21st century.

Accordingly, this book suggests putting the "human" at the centre. The human is, in the very end, the source of social norms, legal norms, and technical standards. This does not mean that one individual creates them. It means reconsidering not only the substance of the design of the digital technology (which is the shape the technological architecture will take), but also the method adopted to engage all the stakeholders in the design: this is justified, ultimately, by the fact that human beings are holders of precious knowledge, and the combination of the knowledge of many, if made according to a sound method of policy design and implementation assessment, may lead to better results not only in terms of performance, but also in terms of responsiveness. That is the meaning we associate here to the concept of governance.

In the following pages, digital technology is not treated as "technological fact". The recent transformations undergone by the justice systems, and the outbreak of the intensive application of computation within the realm of law and justice call (all these phenomena together) for a rewording and a reconceptualization. Instead of speaking separately of digital technologies and computation applied within the justice system, it seems preferable to introduce the category of digital infrastructures and, to some extent, "digital infra-functions".

Information sharing, information management, knowledge embedment into crystalized scripts of tasks inscribed into a software, writing and interpreting, all these functions are parts of systems of interactions that take a distinctive connotation when they are performed within a justice system. Digital technologies reshuffle the way these functions are performed by devoted and specialized structures – such as organizational units, services, and roles within the justice courthouses and in the law firms. Moreover, digital technologies inject a new way of writing information and channeling knowledge and contents from one actor to another, from one source to another, and from one organization to another. Tasks that are directly related to the specific nature of the digital technology need to be integrated into a broader array of tasks that have for a long time been traditionally and repetitively performed within micro and macro patterns of behaviours. This is the reason "infra-functions" are permeating functions performed traditionally by the justice systems. The sum of the traditional functions, determined by compliance to the civil and penal procedural laws, to the routines and the practices of labour and doing things that courts and law firms have developed, and of digitally driven new functions is much more than the simple aggregation of "n + n" items (this means in practical terms that we cannot focus simply on the addition of inputs, such as human resources or technological resources; each input interacts with the other and the overall pattern of interaction can be understood as an addition, rather it looks more like a complex matrix of interdependences). Digital infrastructures are, therefore, stable sets of methods to create order and meaning among actions: they are interlaced with other infrastructures that coexist within the justice systems.

Still, despite the critical role played by digital infrastructures within the transformative processes undergone by the justice systems over the last decades, the "technical" dimension of these processes must not be over-estimated. Beside this, technology and digital infrastructures are not exogenous factors impinging upon a system and influencing the components of this system in a linear, direct, and predictable way. The narrative we need to build is more complex – and maybe more fascinating. By abandoning a genuinely linear understanding of the interaction that technology has with the justice system, one regains the role of the actors, who remain the ultimate and the fundamental engines of change (Lacour and Piana 2019).

Delivering justice for all and ensuring responsive governance of the justice sector are concerns shared by most of the countries in the world. Beyond the different cultural legacies and the institutional settings, societies seem to agree upon the overarching function justice performs by creating either favourable or non-favourable conditions to the enforcement of fundamental rights and thereby making true the promise of the rule of law: this means equal treatment in the actual protection of individual rights.

How this takes place, the extent to which extra-judicial and judicial spaces contribute, each of them, to deliver better justice for all, and the capacity to make the best out of the scientific and technological advancements we are all facing today, remains in the hands of the decision-makers to shape and define.

The call for action that consequently arises is more a call for an architectural design of the digital infrastructures than a call for marginal adaptation.

Exogenous factors that have unexpectedly triggered new waves of changes within the justice system. Among several new forces that have emerged within our societies, digital technologies and the interlaced data science achievements, in terms of artificial intelligence, automation, and internet of things, are unquestionably the most disruptive ones both for the trust people grant to legal services providers, and for the role the rule of law plays in regulating people's daily life.

The process of decoupling structures from functions that incorporate digital technologies may go very far: the components of the structures set up to treat the demand of justice in a material space are dematerialized and then reframed in different structural settings.

The example of mediating rituals among litigants transformed into online mediation services delivered through a semi-automated device provides one first example of a much broader array of phenomenological innovations, all of them inspired by deep and not yet comprehensively assessed expectations and ideas about what it means to have a response to a demand for justice.

The key takeaways of this book have been thought to benefit policy makers, practitioners, experts, consultants, and opinion leaders, as well as stakeholders that play a role in the amazingly new scenario depicted above.

The main point here is the following: digital infrastructures, penetrating, and interlacing legal structures and judicial institutions do not represent a marginal adjustment to a consolidated paradigm of governance. They require instead a paradigm shift in the method by means of which practice-driven know-how, case-driven assessment, research, and economic interests are implicated right at the beginning of a circle of governance that involve regulators, monitoring bodies, the public, and the research and development (R&D) (Jarrahi and Nelson 2018). This must be done while overcoming the traditional public-private divide on the side of learning and monitoring, whereas the regulative role must be safely situated in the hands of the public. This entails a policy of engagement as well as transparency. The new compass outlined in the final chapter formalizes and provides the details of the model that embeds these ideas.

As for all books inspired by a vision and passionate engagement, this owes its keystones to a fortunate moment, notably, the chance of attending the OECD meeting hosted in Lisbon in 2018 where the cutting-edge between ICT infrastructures and automated mechanisms of justice administration and legal services delivery appeared more as a puzzle than as a clear line. As a matter of fact, in the setting of an international dialogue unfolding among technical and political actors the key subject at a glance was the transformation justice and legal institutions are experiencing. This is a consequence of the technological and scientific advances touching both hard- and software as well as the computational capacities handled with unexpected effectiveness and performance by new devices.

The ICT and the computational developments that we all are observing today worldwide are presumably a compelling reason to pivot on the notion of the justice system, to reconsider and to value the demand of legal and justice services, and to re-centre on people – rather than on models – the design of the policies that are strongly and vocally requested to ensure that justice is a field whose quality is strengthened by the digital transformation under reinforced conditions of institutional accountability, transparency, and responsiveness to citizens. This needs to take place in a world, under conditions of continuous trustworthiness.

People must gain the centre of the agenda

Echoing from the other side of the globe, two friends are having a coffee and sharing their concerns about the settlement of a dispute. "I have just discovered that the entrance to my house has been damaged and now I will need to pay for the tenant's carelessness and lack of attention to the property. I'm wondering if it is worth the time-consuming, uncertainty and expensive burdens of civil litigation? Yet, I feel dutybound when it is a matter of individual freedoms and rights!" The friend replies: "Why don't you try to reach a solution using algorithms?" This sounds like a viable solution: "Algorithm? I would never risk a legal outcome by putting it in the hands of algorithms!" The friend responds in a more detailed manner:

> Well algorithms do not have hands nor hearts, they do not have preferences nor attitudes they simply brutally calculate and come up with an objective neutral and reliable response. These are based on the probability of getting the costs back that you have been forced to pay to repair your house and they will come up with the best legal options. Algorithms can provide all this.

This would seem exactly the most suitable avenue to the settlement of a dispute that a person could ask for. "Wow! Does this mean that I wouldn't even need a lawyer? And for sure a neutrally objective method of calculation would be very reassuring. Let's go for it! Just a marginal issue: who creates the algorithms?" Shadows start to cast: "Well that's too complicated I really don't know ...". This is the point where practical wisdom comes in: "uhm ... and how do we know that the algorithm is trustworthy?"; "Well we do not know at all but they say that this is intelligence, artificial in its nature but always intelligence ..." answers the friend. "But can we class something as intelligent if we do not understand how it works?" wonders the other.

Is this story pure fantasy or rather the kind of common situation experienced in daily life? For several reasons, among which the search for greater efficiency and more accessibility are prominently highlighted, digital devices for the administration and delivery of justice are rapidly and relentlessly becoming a priority for policy makers, domestic and international institutions, regulators, legal experts, and consultants. Changes triggered by the encounter between technological tools and justice institutions are countless and span a wide range of dimensions, including procedural, substantial, organizational, communicational, which all together impinge upon the way rights are protected and enforced. In a sense, the arrival of technology has been welcomed by the many who unveiled the failures of the state in providing timely and efficient responses to the demands of services coming from citizens, social groups, and companies. In a more nuanced manner, for the large plethora of critics of the opacity, lack of efficiency, low performance, and poor accountability of public administration, e-justice seems to make true the dream of a slimmed down public sector where human ways of doing things is replaced by more efficient and reliable rationality: that of the digits (Contini and Mohr 2009).

Digital rendition of information went hand in hand with the advancement of the platforms that channel, record, and enable the retrieval of such information once decoupled from the source of its digitalization. In this respect, digitalization is a social process that takes place within and through a social medium, unfolds through, and because the social humus, instantiated by actors, organizations, professionals, methods of doing things that intervene all along the process. In the justice system, digital devices and digital rendition of information anticipated and paved the way for the entry of digital infrastructures and digital functions, which have reshaped the behaviour, expectations, choices, and ultimately the language. The social nature of this phenomenon can be fully understood once it is observed and investigated through the lens offered by the concept of intelligence. Intelligence is a theory-dense concept, featuring an unquestionable normative dimension. None would argue that "being intelligent" is not a good thing. Still, Paul Valery was right when he stated that "intelligence is one of those notions that derive all their value from the other terms coupled with them by affinity or contrast, in some discourse" (Valery 1962 (original 1925)). Intelligence is, though, a very promising heuristic to disentangle the interplay between legal professionalism, organizational practices embedded in the justice institutions, and the rationalities that are at play within the computational devices applied to law cases and legal analytics. Here we adhere to the idea promoted by Agenda 2030. According to Geoff Mulgan, digital technology has the merit of unveiling the cognitive processes that lie at the basis of social living. In the following pages this idea is taken as a heuristic to better understand this interplay and to prospect the model of governance that may be more responsive, inclusive, and legitimate for the justice systems that integrate the "digital": "the intelligence has something to do with the 'whom we choose to collaborate with' and with the 'how we act under which conditions'" (Mulgan 2017). Part of the answer relies on the reflexive rationality: the choice. Part of the answer also relies on practical competence: routines, tacit knowledge, and so on. The arrival of the digital reshapes all these aspects and dimensions.

In a way, it looks like an unpredicted and unpredictable encounter of intelligence(s).

If this reasoning is correct, it enables us to meet the "artificial intelligence", that is, the science that investigates the behaviour of agents that can perceive the environment and can perform actions. In the public discourse that reaches out the broad audience – not the audience of specialized professionals – words associated with artificial intelligence (AI) cover a "menu" of techniques, such as data mining, profiling, and machine learning. This latter simulates a learning process driven from the recursive application of computational rationality to a set of data that is selected from a massive dataset. The word "machine" aims to point to the automated nature of the learning process. The word "learning" emulates the meaning humankind associates with the growth of adaptive capacity to the environment. However, data mining and profiling feature critical aspects if applied to the legal and justice sector.[4]

For almost one century the justice system and artificial intelligence have lived their lives separately. The encounter begins in the early decade of the 21st century when the application of computational rationalities to the digitalized contents of legal documents and judicial acts rendered in digital terms made it possible to elaborate, with an unprecedented efficacy, information about trends, patterns, and regularities.

By taking the epistemological posture, similar to the wearing of multi-focal lenses, we observe both actors following and developing forms of intelligence and, by means of the interactions of those, setting up organizational forms of intelligence. This epistemological posture offers a precious epistemic value: one that allows us more comprehensively to assess the role played within the justice systems by both digital technologies and computational rationalities. Both of these are kinds of intelligence – embedded into the ICT devices, platforms, and so on,

---

4 See Borgesius 2019 for a comprehensive portrait of these techniques. Profiling judges and lawyers calls for urgent regulative intervention, preventing the interference within the autonomous sphere of these actors. Still the application of this technique, enabled by the availability of dataset in digital format on the decisions taken by these actors, may respond to a social need of more homogeneity and therefore be easily accepted as a way to medicate the lack of equal treatment. Given the sensitivity of the potential effects for the guarantees of professional autonomy and judicial independence, in some countries regulative acts have been adopted to prevent this practice. This is the case in France, for instance, where a law was adopted in 2019 whose key article (33) reads: "The identity data of magistrates and members of the judiciary cannot be reused with the purpose or effect of evaluating, analysing, comparing or predicting their actual or alleged professional practices".

and within the rationales put into motion in the processes of machine learning and, more generally, in the data analytics applied to case laws and legal documents.

The loss of sharpness that comes from the cross-disciplinary categorization of these two kinds of intelligence – the first better grasped by technological engineering and the second one by applied mathematics and the information sciences – is compensated by the gain in terms of perspective when this categorization is used to engage in the design of a new method of governance. When we speak about the justice system a new compass is needed to help us govern the entire digital transformation and all the potential developments that this latter may trigger: this includes the application of powerful computational devices and processes of machine learning to the data that digitize legal texts, judicial behaviour, judicial decisions, legal arguments, and so on.

By taking this epistemological stance, we claim for the abandonment of the dichotomy human versus artificial. One may word the shift from "human" to "artificial" intelligence (Pasquali 2018) as a reductionist turn: human reasoning – based on highly qualified expertise – carried on under the constraints and the protection of the constitutional and procedural guarantees of fair trial and due process of law is now reduced to the numb calculation of a number of inputs typed into digits, filed into a machine and processed by an algorithm. No emotions, no discrimination, no extra costs, no extra-time waiting, no frustration. A completely different way to tell the same story would probably cast light upon the monster that is marching into the justice system Wittkower 2018, subverting the long-standing guarantees of fair trial and disanchoring the administration of justice from the context where it is expected to be rooted and finally legitimated.

However, on closer inspection, the whole story is more complex, encompassing a vast array of aspects with none of them bound to simple efficiency, however important it might be. Modernizing justice institutions, differentiating conflict settlement mechanisms, and redesigning the matrices where demands and offers of justice meet entails much more than simply increasing the speed of case management, reducing the costs of access to justice, and making the justice system transparent – in as much as it becomes readable and open – to non-legal experts. This book aims to cast light on these aspects by means of a framework that places at the centre the citizen and the trust she is ready to grant to the legal and justice mechanisms. The book takes inspiration from a large number of qualitative analyses and in-depth studies in different Member States of the EU and at different levels of jurisdictions.

Today we need a comprehensive and equally courageous approach, which enables us to go beyond the maintenance of the current paradigm. We need to challenge the categories of access, equality, fairness, to dig deeper into the way citizens experience fairness, equality, and access to mechanisms of rights protection, and to recognize to what extent the law/society matrix is totally transfigured by this very recent and yet very powerful innovation.

Here we are reminded of some examples coming out of a much wider phenomenology. Recently, the Los Angeles Police Department adopted a method to predict crime behaviour propensity on the basis of the data analytics applied to the big dataset on individual behaviour, typical situations, and descriptive mindset accounts for types of social actors. This case proved to be very controversial and it testifies to the need for a widely aware and responsive use of AI within the legal and justice system.

Back in 2013, Professor Joel Caplan of Rutgers School of Criminal Justice highlighted that the approach described above keeps in mind short-term objectives. Police officers are able to prevent criminal activities in a particular area, only to allow it to occur elsewhere. Alternatively, the potential criminals return once the police officers leave. Therefore, a more sustainable way would be to perform risk terrain mapping. The crime history of a certain region is merged with local behaviours to define crime-prone areas, thus taking into account the impact of the environment as well. This goes far beyond the pure case management adopted by the courts to speed up the trial time frame or simply to ensure that this is kept under the control of a quality (i.e. efficiency- and effectiveness-oriented) management. In the UK and the Netherlands the tools of "Online Dispute Resolution" have been adopted and many scholars and practitioners have argued for the great potential these mechanisms offer.

In 2016 the Supreme Court of Wisconsin, judging on the use of the Compass software (a software incorporating an algorithm to assess the recidivism risk), stated that this type of tool may be used by judges but cautioned that the reliability of the risk scores provided by the algorithm is necessary. The Compass case triggered a worldwide debate: who is responsible for the final decision on sentencing under the mixed conditions of "intelligence", human and artificial, human reasoning and algorithm-driven analysis? Should algorithms be admitted as subjects of judicial scrutiny? And if we do, how should judicial actors and legal experts keep up with the increasing asymmetry of knowledge that marks the field of data analytics and predictive justice, where the data business and the data scientists are the ultimate holders of the critical expertise that creates awareness and therefore power about the nature, the scope, and the validity of the data analytics devices? The knowledge that can be drawn from massive data sets of cases of civil or commercial litigations, or eventually of criminal cases tells us of the correlations of situations-behaviours-judicial decisions. Patterns of behaviour of litigants-lawyers-judges can be detected and made known to the broad public. Algorithms are expected to tell us the probability of one legal decision or a judicial adjudication of a case that can be set at one point (which is marked by a level of costs, damage repair, fees, punishment, monetary sanction, etc.).[5] It is important for us and for future generations that we examine the wider picture.

This book takes up a challenging and still fascinating endeavour: it maps the practices of digital innovation experienced within the domestic justice systems in the European Member States, it disentangles the dimensions of the artificial intelligence and digital devices applied to the justice sector and it assesses the transformative potential this has, not only in terms of efficiency, accessibility, and readability, but also in terms of actual quality delivered to citizens. To do so, the chapters that follow elaborate first on an analytical grid which integrates three dimensions of the justice system, respectively related to the procedures, the contents, and the outcomes. Notably, the grid aims at helping scholars and practitioners to assess the impact of AI and digital devices against three criteria: the protection of the constitutional and procedural guarantees of a fair trial, the effective delivery of dispute settlements in due time and in an understandable and accessible manner, and the strength of the trust citizens and social groups are ready to grant to the institutions of justice. This first endeavour provides the reader with a multi-spectrum prism to observe the new practices and experiences that are rapidly growing and spreading across courts, institutions, national systems, and regimes of regulations (think for instance of the arbitration at international level in private law).

The journey offered to the reader is inspired by a general hypothesis lying at the basis of the entire analysis, empirical as well as institutional. In times of disruptive change, knowledge often grows within new experiences, in the ground-breaking practices, in frames adopted by change agents. Therefore, we need to know which aspects of the justice system are challenged, transformed, strengthened by artificial

---

5 The different degree of appropriateness of AI tools as they are applied in different legal fields and to different types of litigation is acknowledged by the European Ethical Charter on the use of artificial intelligence in judicial systems and their environment (pp. 41 and 51).

intelligence and digital devices through an empirically oriented and methodologically grounded approach.

Mapping the potential is not a theoretical exercise. This means in practice engaging all actors belonging to the legal and justice eco-system into a structured dialogue with all actors belonging to the digital technology eco-system.

It will highlight the importance of a participative and multiple-voiced approach to the standard setting process, as a drive to increase awareness and transparency. The book takes neither a blindly positive nor a negative stance on AI and digital technology. It is rather inclined to endorse a critical view and an empirically oriented approach to set up a participative, sustainable, and evidence-informed process of regulation for governments, international organizations (IOs), and NGOs. This is because the ultimate beneficiary of the IT must be, not surprisingly, the citizen.

References

Avgerou, C. and Madon, S. "Reframing IS studies: Understanding the social context of IS innovation", in *The Social Studies of Information and Communication Technology*, edited by C. Avgerou, C. Ciborra, and F. Land, Oxford: Oxford University Press, 2004.

Capoccia, G. "Critical junctures and institutional change", in *Advances in Comparative Historical Analysis*, edited by J. Mahoney and K. Thelen, Cambridge: Cambridge University Press, 2015, pp. 147–179.

Commaille, J. *A Quoi nous sert le droit?* Paris: Gallimard, 2015.

Commaille, J. *L'Esprit Sociologique des Lois*, Paris: PUF, 1994.

Contini, F. and Mohr, R. "Reconciling independence and accountability in judicial systems", *Utrecht Law Review*, 2009, 3(1).

Council of Europe, European Ethical Charter on the use of artificial intelligence in the judicial systems and their environment, Strasbourg, Office for Official Publication, 2018.

De Monticelli, R. *Al di qua del bene e del male*, Torino: Einaudi, 2015.

Ewick, P. and Silbey, S.S. *The Common Place of Law*, Chicago and London: The University of Chicago Press, 1998.

Forum, World Economic. "Understanding the Impact of Digitalization on Society", 2018.

Jarrahi, M. and Nelson, S. "Agency, sociomateriality, and configuration work", *The Information Society*, 2018, 34(4): 244–260.

Koselleck, R. *Krise*, Stuttgart: Klett-Cotta, 1972.

Lacour, S. and Commaille, J. "After legal consciousness studies: Dialogues transatlantiques et transdisciplinaires", *Droit et Société*, demonographic issue, 2019, 100: 543–788.

Lacour, S. and Piana, D. "Faitez Entrer les Algoritmes", *Revue Cités*, 2019, 80: 47–60.

Mulgan, G. *Big Mind*, Princeton: Princeton University Press, 2017.

Pasquali, F. "A rule of persons not machines: The limits of legal automation", *George Washington Law Review*, 2018, 87(1): 1–55.

Piana, D. *Uguale per tutti?* Bologna: Il Mulino, 2016.

Polanyi, M. *The Tacit Dimension of Knowledge*, London: Routledge, 1966.

Valery, P. *The Outlook of Intelligence*, Princeton: Princeton University Press, 1962 (original 1925).

2 Reframing the digital picture

Stories one may read

Caroline has been waiting for the verdict for too long, indeed. In the end, the jury sentenced and she felt relieved. Patently the victim, she was aware that the way towards the discovery of the "judicial truth" resembles a stair, made of proof and evidence taking, hearings and recordings, upsets and regrets.

When the subjective "judicial truth" becomes judicially "true", everything seems suddenly easy and spontaneously settled. Sure, evidences were so patently clear! All these anxieties, all these dramas felt overnight for weeks and weeks, when all the photos published online did not leave much room for interpretation. So what is the point in going through all these steps, she wondered many times! All the procedural duties to establish the truth are really necessary, when the information that one finds on the web about similar cases seems so clear, so immediate, and so final in its verdict? Well, hopefully, all this is over now!

Joseph was sitting in silence, overwhelmed by his frustration. How can it be excusable that the hearing was postponed once again? Well, fine, he filed a minor claim. The awareness that in the courthouses much more serious cases are filed added to his frustration of a feeling of mismatch. Maybe instead of addressing his demand to the court it would have been much better to have searched for different, extra-judicial means. Judges must be very busy, he thought, after sharing a cup of tea with his best friend, Aaron, a legal attorney who was describing the key details of a long and complex judicial affair in commercial law for him: a guy who was desperately trying to regain his legitimacy in running a business after a financial crisis and a budget crush provoked by a nasty and opaque operation managed by one of his commercial partners who had left him in dirty water with banks, creditors, and potential donors. Why should a judge ever take care of Joseph's demand to obtain a simple reimbursement for his tenant's misbehaviour? Are they two comparable things? Joseph was perfectly aware that they are not. And still, he felt that the mere fact of having been postponed, placed second rank, made him feel "discriminated". As a matter of fact, a rapid solution, even less legally sophisticated would have been fine.

Three waves of digital transformation

Technological advancements relentlessly marked the 20th century. Consequently, they cast a new light on the sunrise of the 21st century. Among the countless transformations the outbreak of digital technology in daily life must be acknowledged, without hesitation, as the most disruptive global social fact recorded in contemporary history (Bijker, Hughes, and Pinch 1987). This holds also for the justice systems.

To single out the differential impacts digital technologies endangered within the justice systems, these must be understood as complex matrix of functions, structures, and patterns of interaction. It is worth disentangling the "justice system" into its several components to reach a better understanding of the potential impact technologies have (and may have) on it. In Figure 2.1 these components are portrayed alongside the demand-offer cycle of justice. The components are also pictured in relationship to the timing of the technological reforms that unfolded

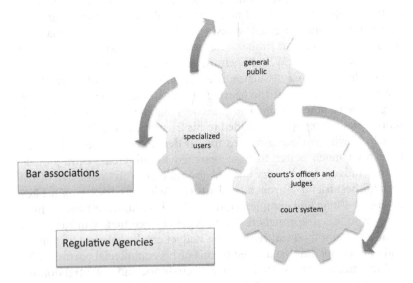

Figure 2.1 Structural components of a justice system

over four decades. The changes triggered through them impinged on law firms/courts interfaces, the management of courts, the clerks'/judges' interactions, the public/courts communications, the regulatory agencies'/territorial structures' (such as appeal courts, first instance courts, specialized jurisdictions) exchanges of information, and the law firms'/bar associations' interactions.

If we keep in mind the structural components illustrated in Figure 2.1, we will achieve a better understanding of the complexity featured by the interlaced waves of reforms that each of these components, or a combination of those, have undergone over the last four decades (Kosar 2017; Burbank, 1999).

This happened due to a number of concomitant reasons. First, the scope of the judicial function has been forced to expand. Increasingly complex and intensive litigations have demanded a deeper and wider response from judicial institutions in many countries and, more importantly, in countries featuring high levels of fragmentation or cultural polarization (Stone Sweet 2000; Morlino and Sadurski 2010). These phenomena have provoked the overload of the judicial institutions and have called for a reallocation of resources within the administrative services attached to them. Second, the economic crisis that hit the Euro-zone in 2007 and 2008 forced public institutions to rethink their human resources endowment and rationalize their spending plans (Morlino 2020).

In the field of justice administration, the extension of the new public management paradigm met favourable conditions to its acceptance. These conditions are political and cultural: they consisted of the increasing critical stance taken by the broad public and political actors towards the lack of efficiency and effectiveness of the courts. In the early 1990s, the quest for better performance urged a review of the organization of the courts. This went through a comprehensive process of rationalization in the budget allocation scheme. In many countries, the role played by IT tools in improving court management has been widely praised under the auspices of an efficiency-oriented approach (Frydman 2011; Jean 2005), which was warmly welcomed to react to the crisis. As a matter of fact, the cost/benefit ratio inspired the policy discourses of the judicial reforms adopted in almost all southern European countries (Piana and Verzelloni 2019; Verzelloni 2017).

Beyond the endowment of IT devices in the courthouses, many dockets have been partly or completely transformed into digital data set. The management of the cases (document filing, document delivering, document sharing and editing) takes place through digital support. This impacts heavily on the work organization within the courts and the subsequent patterns of interaction that unfold between lawyers and courts, the laypeople and the courts, and the courts among them (for instance between first instance and appeal courts).[1]

This comprehensive transformation process relied on the same exogenous factor, digital technology (www.bizcommunity.com/Article/196/706/167197.html), which provided large-scale support for transferring the documental structure that irrigates the daily activities of legal and justice actors from material to impalpable support. It also creates an opportunity to reshuffle the mechanisms by means of individual and organizational interplay (Borgmann 1984; Misa, Brey, and Feenberg 2003). Consequently, a chain of multiple transformations unfolded at court level: "From the moment we introduce a technological mediation, there is a recomposition of professional practices at the hearing".[2]

By encountering digital technology, justice systems deployed a vast array of reactive and proactive strategies, spanning resistance, adaptation, and acclimatization (Christensen and Laegreid 2001), altogether reflecting a certain number of common features to the change patterns already observed and implemented in other policy sectors (Christensen and Laegreid 2001).

Three decades have passed: today we stand in a promising cognitive perspective to 1) identify converging and diverging paths followed by countries in incorporating digital technology in the justice sector; 2) put an emphasis on the key driving mechanisms of change; and 3) put together the puzzle pieces and draw the borders of the empirical field we will delve into in the following pages.

Before doing this, an overview of the state of the art in the member states of the Council of Europe, as offered by the Commission Européenne pour l'Evaluation de l'Efficience des Systèmes Judiciaires, helps paint the overall picture.

Data collected by the CEPEJ are a debated issue: one of the main criticisms points to the gap that unquestionably exists between the de

---

1 It will never be sufficiently stressed the related importance of the quality of the legal drafting in this context. Digitalized documents may be much more easily processed if they feature a standardized or at least a rationalized format. This has been the focus of a number of policy guidelines adopted in the national judicial systems – such as in France or in Italy – and at the level of the district courts – with the format of a protocol signed by the judiciary and the bar. (See on this point www.fondazioneforensefirenze. it/uploads/fff/files/2019/2019_05%20-%20Maggio/20%20-%20La%20motivazione%20 della%20sentenza/Locandina%2020_05_2019.pdf which witnesses the engagement of all justice actors into a participative project aiming at setting guidelines about the quality of legal drafting.)

2 www.pacte-grenoble.fr/sites/pacte/files/files/dpn1806entretiendumoulin.pdf.

jure provisions fixing the terms of the ICT tools used by the courts and the de facto socialization of legal and judicial actors of these tools in the daily practice. However, one major point can be safely claimed on the basis of the overall state of the art represented by the figure above. This refers directly to the wide and uncontested salience of the digital issue in the justice systems of all CoE members. Furthermore, a consistent majority of CoE member states engaged in the "second step" of the IT development, labelled as "phase 2"; the second evidence to be taken consists in a converging pattern of advancement towards the investment on the governance of IT devices; the third aspect that is worth mentioning refers to the predominant category of services, which are tailored to support the daily activity of the judge and, in relation to this, file management and the exchanges of documents between judges and the administrative staff operating within the courthouses.

What has been pursued by enacting this transformation? Digital formats are preferred to paper-based systems; IT is loudly praised as a drive to efficiency and a cost-reduction strategy. Moreover, the possibility to access justice institutions through IT tools (front office through which individuals may file a case or follow-up the case in which they are litigants or convicted) may be an asset for those justice systems that are too dispersed throughout the territory and still cannot count on an effective transport network enabling citizens living in the countryside to move to the main courthouses.

The same picture shows the differential paths followed by the countries. Already in the early 2000s we observed two dominant change patterns: one, featured by civil law countries, where the bulk of IT development dealt with court management and, thereby, prospected a result-oriented response to the crisis of efficiency and performance of the judicial systems.[3] Here the focus was more on the court systems, that is, on the supply side of the justice sector, with a strong emphasis put on the potential impact that IT development was expected to have on the rationalization of the public expenditure schemes. If this observation is coupled with the economic crisis that hit the sovereign debts in the 2007 and in the 2008, the rationale of e-justice emerges as furtherance of the

---

3 It is worth noting that the waves of change that have been impacting the national judicial systems have been not concomitant in the countries. If we take the spectrum of the countries that are members of the Council of Europe we observe that in the Northern European countries these transformations took place earlier than in the Southern European countries, where the 2007 and 2008 economic crisis played as the catalyst of a pervasive wave of reforms aimed at ensuring the efficiency and the performance of the judiciary. (See on this CEPEJ, 2018 and on the differences between the European countries Piana, 2020.)

already sketched out strategy of judicial reforms that aim at maximizing performance. In countries where the justice sector has been traditionally structured on a different balance between society and the state, a compound policy agenda, focusing on IT development, but covering both sides, the demand and the supply, made its appearance in the early 2000s. Accordingly, the policies adopted impinged upon the legal services provided to social groups and citizens. This part of the agenda ranks in those domestic contexts where demands for a legal response to a social or an economic problem have not traditionally found a first and exclusive path to a qualified – and specialized – response through the court system. In the late 2000s the application of technological devices also conquered the demand side in most countries.

And yet, beyond these diverging paths, on the macroscale the waves of changes that have influenced the justice sectors, due to and triggered by the advancements in digital technology, may be split into three waves.

First wave of reforms. This first wave of IT-driven judicial reforms has largely impinged upon both the organizational and the procedural components of the justice systems. As a matter of fact, the way in which cases are managed, files are filed, documents are drafted, shared and delivered, represents just a first, even though not irrelevant, target level of the IT impact on justice administration. At first, courthouses were foremost influenced by the technological platforms hosting their repositories, the exchange of communications and transactions of documents with the legal firms based on the website and eventually by the possibility offered by technology to adopt a team-working method. The rationale of this (long and still ongoing round of judicial reforms) was efficiency. Digital technology has penetrated the organizational matrix which embeds the practices and the know-how, scripts and routines by which continuity is ensured beyond the judicial staff turn-over: Courtroom technology has broadly been defined as: "any system or method that uses technology in the form of electrical equipment to provide a clear benefit to the judicial process" (CEPEJ 2014).

More specifically, the various technologies used by the courts can include IT equipment such as laptops, iPads, court recording, transcription and video/audio conferencing technology; as well as administrative software such as case management systems, e-filing systems, e-libraries, case laws dataset and sentencing support systems (Donoghue 2017). The mantra was to modernize the courthouses and to allow a more timely and less costly production of the response parts in civil, criminal, and, to a certain extent, administrative cases that were required of the justice systems.

Second wave of reforms. From organization management to case management and backwards. A new season was rising at the end of 2000 as proceedings were progressively transferred from paper to a digital format. This happened with differential trajectories and at a different pace in the countries, depending on the institution that came first in de-materializing the procedures. In France, for instance, this took place first at the level of the supreme courts, both in the Council of State and in the Supreme Court of Cassation. The path followed by the French system reveals the key components of a distinctive pattern of change management. In the 2000s, the two supreme jurisdictions engaged in a comprehensive process of de-materialization of civil and administrative procedures, led by a pilot work developed in a "cooperative policy arena" (Dallara and Piana 2015). The Bar Association that serves in the two supreme courts played the role of catalyst for cooperation, linking the two processes of change management.[4] These processes unfolded in a coupled and coordinated manner. The opposite path characterized the Italian system, in which the external influence exerted by the European Court of Human Rights of Strasbourg, which sanctioned the country for the violations of article 6, and the domestic pressure that broke out in the promotion of a constitutional amendment by which the "right to a fair trial" was entrenched among the constitutions provisions in 2001, created altogether favorable conditions for the rise of a new policy window in which the de-materialization of the civil procedure was launched. This did not take place at the national level. Rather, by merging the initiative of some championing chief justices with the availability of resources – structural and economic – by the District Bar Associations, the first experiences of digital civil procedure made their appearance in Milan, Florence, and Bologna and progressively expanded in the country (Piana forthcoming). Only in 2014 did the Ministry of Justice, with a law decree, make digital civil procedures compulsory and, subsequently, the extension of the same software adopted in the first instance court to the appeal courts and to the Supreme Court of Cassation.

In the Netherlands, since the early 2000s, a very large, open, and up-to-date database including the case law for all Dutch courts has progressively been set up. For the judgments, judges use automated formats that fill in all formalities (names, dates). In order to guarantee textual and material uniformity, law clerks – who actually write the decisions, at least in criminal cases – use automated 'building blocks'. These can be standard sentences from statutes. But judges also have lots of building

---

4 A framework agreement has been signed in 2007 https://rm.coe.int/table-ronde-gerer-efficacement-les-taches-au-sein-de-la-cour-de-cassat/1680792bac#_Toc374451343.

blocks that are quotes from important Supreme Court judgments. While preparing cases, law clerks use automated forms, which contain flow diagrams of legal cases. These diagrams indicate which legal issues need extra attention and what steps need to be taken. All of this does not mean that the judgments don't contain legal reasoning, but to some extent judges have automated the process of decision writing. The role of criminal and administrative judge role is to correct conceptual decisions. There is now some discussion about the importance of the role of law clerks.[5] There is an internal Wiki Juridica that can only be reached by court members and which contains in-depth information and internal memos from all courts. All judges and law clerks have their own highly secure laptop connected to their court system, which does not need Wi-Fi but has a 4G connection, which allows them to work anywhere, at any time, also abroad. Having this context as a background, the trajectories followed to introduce IT innovations take specific significance concerning the role played by leaders in the Dutch judicial system.

Since 2002, a comprehensive reform led by central institutions has been designed and subsequently implemented. It involved the appeal courts, the judicial school, the new Council of the Judiciary, the evaluation and monitoring mechanisms of the court management, to mention but only some of the several aspects touched by the reformers. Chief justices have been part of the "constellation of actors" involved in the reform implementation, having the responsibility to make the best of it and to translate legal devices into practical patterns of behaviour. The first aspect that deserves attention is the role played in the interface between central institutions and the court. As the system gives room for manoeuvre to the courts about the way they manage the budget and pursue strategies of quality of justice, the managerial accountability and the institutional accountability are interlaced. The evaluation of the chiefs depends on the results achieved in terms of court management. This has become even more prominent in the context of the recently introduced IT reforms. The first one stems from a scientific initiative taken by the University of Twente with the support of the Hague Institute for the Internationalisation of the Law. It consists of an IT device that allows the user and the legal representative to interact through a completely dematerialised system. Through the platform, the user can receive several legal services, such as triage, counselling, mediation, and follow-up during the executive phase.

---

5 A recent dissertation focuses on that aspect: www.uva.nl/content/nieuws/persberichten/2017/08/de-griffier-administratieve-ondersteuner-of-invloedrijke-adviseur.html.

Under the influence of the positive but still limited effects obtained, a further innovation has been adopted, this time with the engagement of some chief justices. In 2013, the Ministry for Justice and Security, in partnership with the Council of the Judiciary, launched a new program of modernization which comprises the mandatory digital procedure for civil and commercial proceedings. While the lead of the reform is in the hands of the central institutions, at least from the point of view of political accountability, at the local level chief justices are involved both in the team that designs the innovations and in the team responsible for the implementation. The trajectory followed is divided into steps. A first stage is experimental in its own nature, both in terms of courts applying the new system and in terms of substantial matters touched by it. Interviews made at the level of the appeal chief justices made it clear that the involvement of the leaders of the courts in the design was crucial to make this initiative into a lever of change in the daily life of the courts.

A similar pattern is followed by the Belgian system. Some years ago Belgium adopted an ambitious digitalization program named Phoenix. This was to digitalize the entire set of judicial proceedings and all documents delivered or exchanged within the court system. The failure of this initiative led the central institutions to adopt a different approach, which can be qualified as "integrated and modular". The new IT reform plan envisages a first stage of experimentation which goes hand in hand with a process of participatory design of the reforms and a focus on the functions, role, and rituals that are featured by all actors and organizations operating in the justice system. In this respect, the follow-up of the IT reform requires the chief justices to participate in the design stage and their commitment in the implementation stage.

Even under different institutional conditions due to the constitutional architecture in common law systems, the arguments unfolded above also apply to the judiciary in England and Wales, where the current court reform program "Transforming our Justice System" includes a £1 billion plan to modernize the court system. This involves an investment of £700 million by the Ministry of Justice to reform and modernise the courts and the tribunal system. This is in addition to £270 million made available to develop a fully connected criminal courtroom by 2020.[6]

Third wave of reforms. During the 2000s, a progressive shift of the target pursued by policy makers in reforming the justice system must be acknowledged. This put at the core of the institutional agenda the

6 See: https://consult.justice.gov.uk/digital.../transforming...courts.../consultationpaper. pdf.

interaction between users – and their representatives – and the court systems. A further emphasis on the accessibility of the mechanisms of dispute settlement was put on the technological potential in which ADR started to get more legitimacy and visibility:

> As communication and commerce between distant parties became widespread, a growing number of disputes emerged for which courts and ADR processes provided no feasible avenue of redress ... the new generation ODR processes came to celebrate the unique qualities of online interaction and the shifts associated with the transition to digital means of addressing conflict: the shift from physical to online communications, the shift from a human "third party" to the "fourth party," and the shift from a "data-less" mentality to processes that revolve around data.
>
> (Katsh and Rabinovich-Einy 2017)

For years we have been told that IT may reduce costs and increase freedom for citizens. Even though we would not argue the opposite, the relationship between IT injection – included IT embedded into algorithms applied to the justice systems – and equality is far from genuine. IT can drive more equality to access information. This is what is provided through the so called French SAUJ. SAUJ is a front desk set up at the level of the first instance courts in France, where citizens can get free information orientation and access to the cases where they are the litigants, victims, witnesses, or the convicted. It plays a simplified mechanism in access to the justice system. Introduced in France as an experimental practice in 2014 and followed in a sample of pilot courts from 2014 and 2016 (Bobigny, Brest, Dunkerque, Privas, Saint Denis de la Réunion, and Vesoul), this has been extended to the national court system.

The introduction of the SAUJ impacts upon the scope of action of the chief justices, notably in terms of strategies that have been encouraged to adopt in order to strengthen the public accountability of the courts. This means that citizens may be empowered to follow and verify what courts do in terms of resource management, timeframes, and organization. And yet SAUJ does not tell the entire story about the magnitude and the disruptive (positive or negative is a matter to be debated and in fact it is climbing fast and furiously to the top spot concerning being breaking news in the public debate) of the new justice reform agenda put forth by the French Garde des Sceaux Nicole Belloubet. The extension of the online mediation procedure to cases traditionally handled and adjudicated by the first instance judge – notably the jurisdiction devoted to small claims and misdemeanours – calls for not only the attention of scholars and practitioners, but also of citizens and all holders of social and collective rights.

Overall, the three waves of reforms (Piana forthcoming), if assessed as a whole, regardless of the differential paths followed and the different time frames, offer an overview of the role played by technological advancements within the justice sector. As a matter of fact, technology did not perform the function of a structural variable, directly and linearly impinging upon the way justice systems are organized, allocated resources and establish a connection between expected results and the demands of services and responses. The interplay model is more complex and calls for a different understanding than the one promoted by a purely efficiency-centred approach. The European Justice Scoreboard provides an eloquent portrait of the trends featured by European member states in the adoption and implementation of policies focusing on the potential embedded in digital infrastructures, both in organizational terms – mostly in the court management – and in terms of communication – mainly in the interplay between the court and users, laypeople, and professionals.

Patently, the overall distribution of ICT within the court systems impinged upon one of the key dimensions of the quality of justice, the management of the daily workload. ICT are both highly instrumental in case management and court efficiency control by means of automated statistics and data retrievals. By shifting to the digital format, court judgments and decisions have become much more easily accessible in many countries.

This proves the extent to which managerial and digital turns have unfolded in an interdependent pattern of change, featuring a mutually reinforcing interaction. Once translated into digits, judicial documents require a different management, which consequently enables a new data analysis.

Digital technology performed as a catalyst for change in two different manners. On the one hand, and in some systems, technology creates new policy windows where actors, with reputational resources, leadership, and situated in a high rank within the system, have been enabled to pursue the improvements they aimed at in terms of better organization. On the other hand, technology impinged upon the benefit-cost ratio of some new organizational and communication options, such as web-mediated e-filing, web-mediated accountability of court performance, functional differentiation of e-filing, and document delivery for different demands and needs and different social groups. But a "fil rouge" links up all these happenings: the lack of a preliminary and systemic compass to govern the development, use, and impact of the digital transformation. This would have required a structural and institutionalized method of governance comprising the entire policy design and implementation cycle, with a strong emphasis on the monitoring and learning from practices phase. This is just to say, in a nutshell, that digital transformations entail the rise of the agency,[7] as a driving mechanism of change and, consequently, as a key pillar in a new compass for a more responsive and comprehensive governance method.

The fourth dimension: artificial intelligence coming in

If these changes are reframed in the general context of the transformation of the demands that citizens and communities address to the legal and justice institutions, we could get a certain number of hints about the policy discourse that lies at the origin of what we can qualify as a "digital turning point" in the justice sector: citizen-oriented legal and justice services are crucial for the economic development; dematerialized mechanisms of dispute resolution may be more effective, but they can also jeopardize the perception of comprehensibility and intelligibility that historically and traditionally have been context-tailored or socially embedded mechanisms of dispute resolution; new professionalisms are requested in a IT-based system of justice administration; credibility and transparency are necessary for the quality of justice delivered to citizens; efficiency-oriented reforms are not per se capable to irreversibly increase the level of citizens' trust in judicial institutions.

The crisis of citizens' trust in legal and justice institutions represents a distinctive mark in the late 20th and the dawn of the 21st century. This phenomenon, which occurs on a macro scale, takes its origin from the interplay of three legacies, each of them related to the above mentioned waves of judicial reforms.

The first legacy dates back to the managerial turn which hit the public sector. The transition did not take place exclusively in the policy discourse and, thereby, in the tools and blueprints, managed to make the wish of a more effective and efficient public sector come true. This shift is equally mirrored in the expectations of stakeholders and societies. Citizens started to adhere to widely accepted beliefs, which identify the cause of the bureaucratic inefficiency with the hyper-proceduralisation of the administrative acts. This ended with the promising horizon of a renewed public sector in which the rationale was pivoting around the

---

7 The notion of agency and its differential components are the subject of the next chapter.

quest for a new organizational setting where standards and quantitative measuring were about to become the healing wind that renews the way in which law and society interact.

The second legacy arises from the expansion of the litigation deriving from the de-structuring process that affected the traditional mechanisms of intra-organizational regulation, the increase of social and economic mobility, and the fragmentation of the communities where tacit social norms had played for decades, if not centuries, the role of conflict-preventing mechanisms. The high number of cases that started to be filed in the courts, with different emphasis in different countries, but certainly in all advanced democracies, represented a great challenge for the efficiency of the court systems. If, on the one hand, providing more resources to respond to the request for greater results sounded a non-sustainable strategy, the quest for new forms of legal services, including ADR and ODR,[8] appeared to be a viable solution, on the other.

The third legacy refers to the transformation of the law itself. Without entering into a doctrinal debate that goes far beyond the scope of this book, the complex matrix made up by the combination of several sources of norms, hard and soft laws, as well as the production of a high number of regulative measures that have an impact on the uncertainty and the unpredictability of the economic life of citizens and companies, thereby created a functional vacuum where judicial decisions started to perform a sort of functional substitution. In this respect, the uncertainty of the legal framework – due to the complexity and the fast changing patterns of the statutory and secondary laws – creates favourable conditions for a less homogenous judicial response to the demands of justice.

To conclude without oversimplifying, the response to the demand of justice started to be perceived as arbitrary, inefficient- and not homogeneous, something that suddenly issued a silent and widespread demand for new rationalities that shape legal services and judicial decisions.

The abrupt outbreak of *artificial intelligence* applied to the legal and the justice sector met, in some way, favourable conditions both in terms of organizational context – due to the digital transformations described above – and in terms of social demands and preferences.

Beyond the wide spectrum of theories and notions put forth by scholars and researchers engaged in the development of artificial

---

8 ODR emerged from the synergy between ADR and ICT as a method of resolving disputes arising online and for which the traditional means of dispute resolution were inefficient or unavailable (Cortes, 2010, p. 52).

intelligence tools, a handy and solid understanding of it is provided by Russell and Norvig:

> The main unifying theme is the idea of an intelligent agent. We define AI as the study of agents that receive percepts from the environment and perform actions. Each such agent implements a function that maps percept sequences to actions, and we cover different ways to represent these functions.
>
> (Russell and Norvig 2009)

Artificial intelligence applications are countless and their combination with the wide and unexplored space of digital transformations makes up a first, yet just superficially touched, horizon in 21st-century advancements. A report published in 2019 with the contribution of the United Nations Interregional Crime and Justice highlights that there is an estimated total $152 billion committed toward AI by States. This report is framed into the overall strategy of the UNICRI on AI and robotics.

This is to say that the extent of the actions taken by governmental actors in the field opened by the artificial intelligence renewal which took place in the last ten years is massive. Strategies adopted to promote artificial intelligence developments and applications are mostly inspired by the promise of an unprecedented economic growth and social advancement due to a new combination of intelligences within the organizations, in the institutions, in the market, and in the daily life.[9]

AI tools' applications to the justice sector vary enormously. Without having this as exhaustive account, the following seem to be the most significant – at least if we refer to the study incorporated as an empirical background into the European Ethical Charter for the use of the Artificial Intelligence in the Judicial Systems and in their environment: "advanced case-law search engines; online dispute resolution; assistance in drafting deeds; analysis (predictive, scales); categorisation of contracts according to different criteria and detection of divergent or incompatible contractual clauses; 'Chatbots' to inform litigants or support them in their legal proceedings" (Council of Europe, 2018, p. 17).

---

9 www.forbes.com/sites/cognitiveworld/2019/11/19/the-age-of-thinking-machines/#44645ca41432.

The concomitant influence of facilitating conditions to the widespread AI tools within the justice systems and the exponentially growing potential of data science and information science applied to judicial and legal big data must not be underestimated. Even though countries differ as to their readiness to opt for AI tools within the courts or in support of the court, law firms and ADR providers are largely inclined to explore AI tools' advantages in terms of risk of failure reduction and gain in time and human resources allocation.

What is the takeaway of artificial intelligence as it is applied in the justice sector? Let's start by offering an overview of the artificial intelligence-based tools as they are adopted by legal firms and legal services provided today: they range from different types of organizational and cognitive tools, in some way replacing cognitive operations that are performed in a less efficient manner by human agents and in some other ways integrating working methods and patterns of interactions that traditionally make the distinctive nature of the legal enterprise: digital forensics, case law analytics, drafting tools (Adams 2013), recording devices, automated risk assessment, and prospective diagnosis of the case. Commenting on these applications, Richard Susskind goes as far as to word the consequences of this revolution in terms of the end of lawyers – and maybe of traditional lawyering (Susskind 2013). The disruptive impact of artificial intelligence on the expectations and the prospects that arise within societies in terms of responses to their demands of justice is even more revolutionary if we take the angle of the applications – and the promised applications – in the judicial systems.

Let's offer some examples, notably having in mind the most sensitive fields of justice administration for the broad public and the disadvantaged groups.

Small claims are suitable to an intensive application of automated systems of dispute settlement: they are easily standardized and therefore treated by preset formats such as the one provided by an automated computing device; they are numerous and therefore a different treatment in terms of resources allocated to the services devoted to respond to them seems to adapt to the broad request of faster and more efficient justice delivered to all; in several cases they are readdressed to ADR (alternative dispute resolution mechanisms, such as mediation and conciliation), to free resources, time, space, energies, to treat more complex cases, when automated mechanisms appear unfitting and unsuitable. The fate of small demands of justice seems to feature a common trend across cultures and systems: more or less successfully in France, the Netherlands, Italy, Spain, Belgium, the last ten years have been marked by a prominent shift towards ADR to decrease the pressure put on the shoulders of the courts by the increasing demand of justice.[10]

The availability of digitalized dockets where files are managed in digital format through technological architecture is vital for the launch of the algorithm season: algorithms are, in a way, as human beings, they learn, they are trained. This happens by running a massive dataset of case laws in which algorithms unveil and discover patterns of judicial behavior and patterns of social litigations. Only in this way a case can be treated on the basis of the knowledge that an algorithm has been extracted from the application of a mathematical rationality upon a massive set of data:

> ability given to machines to quickly mobilize in natural language the relevant law to deal with a case ... and to anticipate the probabilities of decisions that could occur "could, according to some, without knowing the authorship of this assertion," replace purely and simply a jurisdiction ... by an algorithm.
>
> (Garapon and Lassègue 2017)

There are several reasons supported by promoters of the algorithmic turn into the justice systems: automated computation devices are more efficient, transparent, objective, and reliable than human beings. Even though the criticisms addressed to this optimistic view are multiple, the potential impact of the encounter between artificial intelligence and the intelligence embedded into the justice systems – the capacity to manage a case, an understanding of how a general rule applies to a single case, the management of a collective decision-making process when complex cases are adjudicated by more than one judge, an understanding of the human dimension of sensitive cases in the family law sector, and so on – is still a vast and underexplored domain.[11]

10 In 2016, the UK Civil Justice Council endorsed a comprehensive report portraying the lack of capacity of the court system to meet the demand of justice, especially when it comes from disadvantaged social groups or when it stems from small claims and minor litigious cases. Small and minor here refer to the petty cases that seem to mark the lives of all of us: the neighbour who violates the rules establishing the rights and duties of common spaces in the estate, damages caused by an erroneous dispatch of an item bought on the internet, the list can be expanded and extended and everyone may have examples that feed it. The report encouraged the judicial institutions to open up new solutions, including a small claims resolution system that takes full advantage of the efficiency, rapidity, and predictability of an algorithm-driven dispute settlement.

11 On machine learning and algorithms are the medication to the failing rationality of judges and lawyers see Lassègue and Garapon 2018 and Meniceur 2020.

Despite being a wide and vibrant matter of discussion, the integration of machine learning processes into the justice system features a high potential for renewal, in many respects. Some scholars are inclined to believe that machine learning processes maybe turn out amazingly effective in predicting the judicial decisions (Aletras et al. 2016; Kleinberg et al. 2018). Some other data scientists maintain that the capacity of the algorithms may be insufficient in predicting the orientation of the final rulings, especially in those fields where the case law is not fully stabilized (Tarissan, 2019).[12]

However, artificial intelligence marching into the policy discourse about legal services and the access to justice elicits a demand for a quality of justice that presumably would not have been worded so loudly and clearly without it.

The most critical and still underexplored facet of AI applied to the justice sector refers to the role that the principle of equality plays within the wide scope of possible AI applications. As recalled above, AI's allure is mostly related to three praised aspects: better efficiency (less time to reach a result), higher objectivity (different actors, if supported by AI devices, will follow similar paths to reach similar decisions and therefore will be easily scrutable by – potentially – everyone who is willing to check the process of decision making), and higher guarantee of equal treatment, which means less discrimination. This point is the most controversial and also the most important of all. As a matter of fact, machine learning applied to legal and judicial dataset reproduces in the justice sector the same side effects that intrinsically originated by the very same nature of the technique:

> by exposing so-called "machine learning" algorithms to examples of the cases of interest (previously identified instances of fraud, spam, default, and poor health), the algorithm "learns" which related attributes or activities can serve as potential proxies for those qualities or outcomes of interest.
>
> (Barocas and Selbst, 2016)

The intrinsic features of the machine learning technique clashes with the promise of equal treatment if made without specific and cautious caveat. As the case of COMPAS proves, the discriminating effect of

---

12 Tarissan 2019 highlights the biases that jeopardize the predictive capacity. Lacour and Piana wonder whether the predictability is desirable. Castelli and Piana argue that prediction is a very misleading concept, which must be replaced by prevedibility or possibility (epistemic) to detect stable trends.

the AI tool may come from the process by means of which features selected to train the machine and to put the machine in the conditions of checking and confirming the patterns it recognizes within the data is somehow unavoidable. How then may the institutions operate to ensure the compatibility between AI and equal access to a fair bench?

Here the concept of "equal access" merges two principles: equality before the law and equality of opportunities. Equality before the law is the pivotal principle of the rule of law: laws have their primacy over the will of men if they consider each individual equal to any other. This also applies (and must apply) to those individuals who are rulers. Equality of opportunities points to a different principle and refers instead to the possibility for everyone to have access to the same set of opportunities, regardless of the economic, social, cultural, and linguistic conditions under which she or he acts. If, on the one hand, equality before the law is a procedural principle, on the other hand, equality of opportunity is a substantial principle – the one that refers to which door people are capable to open and go through.

What citizens want from a highly advanced modernized impartial and socially intelligible court system is a fair trial accessible to all. In the misfortunate event that someone succumbs to a litigation, it must be assured that whenever we address to a judge and in any social and economic status, the trial we have will result into a fair response. Yet this way of reasoning seems to fall short of encountering and responding to the challenges faced today by the advances of AI towards justice systems and the demands of justice as they are formulated and elaborated by social actors, companies, people, us. What is missing?

The unreliability of the technological promise

To meet the challenge launched by this question, we need to watch out for the system effects and take seriously the interdependent nature of the justice system. Justice systems live and adapt to societal changes because they stand between innovation and continuity under an overarching vision of what a justice system should mean to a society at a specific moment in the history. Despite the fact that we are very uneasy with the concept of leadership in the justice sector – since at first glance it seems to clash with the ideal principle of impartiality and impersonality – AI is forced to select and draw a line between the parts of the "fairness" that we can expect from the procedures and the organizational machinery and the parts of the fairness that results from: 1) the dialectic encounters of the parts and 2) the vision of the role played by the justice system compared to other conflict resolution systems such as social regulations, ethics, and so on.

One way to make the general statement a practical guideline to orient policy makers is to promote a participatory design process where the combination of automation and human reasoning is made upon a pluralistic and debated discourse involving all actors and all instances. This design method needs leadership, simply because it needs vision. Which balance and which proportion is to be granted to automation versus human decision? To what extent is standardization not only possible, but eventually welcome and desirable in this field? These are the kinds of choices that we would not leave in the hands of a machine; we want to make it a matter for society, for people, in order to guarantee pluralism and public accountability.

However, before addressing this last issue, which represents the central and final proposal of the book, it is worth going back to the premises that lie at the basis of the reforms and the promises made with reference to artificial intelligence. As rightly highlighted by Jacques Commaille, one of the weaknesses of the current approach to justice systems and, more precisely, to judicial reforms, consists in the monolithic and monistic epistemology that inspires the theories of change assumed by the reformers.[13] Even if this remains implicit, each reform relies on a – presumed – valid theory of change that identifies a lever of change on the basis of which the policies adopted may enact the engine of the transformation. If the leverage is identified with the cultural attitudes of legal and judicial actors, the reformers, to achieve a change, may decide to adopt consequent policy tools that target the cultural attitude (such as training, moral suasion, peer review, etc.). If the lever of change is identified in the input/output link – the machine – therefore, the reformers may opt for targeting either the inputs or the machine to ensure better output.

The overview provided in this chapter provides us with strong empirical evidence to conclude that technologies and computational capacities have taken a first rank place within the justice systems over the last decades. Today, justice systems function on the basis of a pervasive endowment of ICT and, in tight relation to this state of the matter, the introduction of computational tools and data-driven devices encounters a wide open path to follow. However, the promise of better justice for all that is, somehow, implicit in the mainstream, requires a more nuanced epistemological attitude which, afterward, must be mirrored

---

13 This point has been highlighted in Commaille (2018).

and translated into a more pluralistic and socially responsive stance in the design and development of a new approach to governance. Policy makers and practitioners who are committed to setting up a better justice system where legal services are offered, among other channels, also by means of the digital infrastructure, are warmly encouraged to take seriously the "residual" portion of "justice" that citizens demand and technology won't provide. This "portion", as we are going to argue in the next chapter, is not so "residual". It is, rather, the very basis of the legitimacy of the justice system. It is because laypeople demand a fair answer to their legal needs that justice systems are expected to respond: this is an empirical question, whose answer must be driven from an empirical view of the link that links legal needs to legal services.

References

Adams, R. Cybercrime and cloud forensics: Applications for investigation processes IGI Global Publisher, 2013.

Aletras, N., Tsarapatsanis, D., Preoţiuc-Pietro, D. and Lampos, V. "Predicting judicial decisions of the European Court of Human Rights: A natural language processing perspective", *PeerJ Computer Science,* 2016, 2:e93, available at: https://doi.org/10.7717/peerj-cs.93

Barocas, S. and Selbst, A. D., "Big Data's disparate impact", *104 California Law Review* 671 (2016), available at: https://dx.doi.org/10.2139/ssrn.2477899

Bijker, W., Hughes, T., and Pinch, T. eds. *The Social Construction of Technical Systems: New Directions in the Sociology and History of Technology,* Cambridge, MA and London: MIT Press, 1987.

Borgmann, A. *Technology and the Character of Contemporary Life,* Chicago: University of Chicago Press, 1984.

Burbank S. B., The Architecture of Judicial Independence, 72 S. CAL. L. REV. 315, 1999.

Campbell, T., *Artificial Intelligence and Overview of State Initiatives,* 2019, Colorado Future Grasp.

CEPEJ, 2018, Ethical Charter for the Use of the Artificial Intelligence in the Judicial Systems and Their Environment, Strasbourg, Official Püblications. https://rm.coe.int/ethical-charter-en-for-publication-4-december-2018/16808f699c

Christensen, T. and Laegreid, P. *New Public Management: The Transformation of Ideas into Practice,* Farnham, UK: Ashgate, 2001.

Cortes, P. Online Dispute Resolution for Consumers in the European Union, London, Routledge, 2010.

Commaille, J. https://www.cairn.info/revue-droit-et-societe-2018-3-page-657.htm" Les Legal Consciousness Studies selon Susan Silbey: une dissonance entre données empiriques et ressources théoriques?, Droit et Société, numéro monographique, After Legal Consciousness Studies: dialogues transatlantiques et transdisciplinaires, N° 100, pp. 657 à 664.

Dallara, C. and Piana, D. *Networking the Rule of Law*, London: Ashgate, 2015.

Donoghue, J. "The Rise of Digital Justice: Courtroom Technology, Public Participation and Access to Justice", *Modern Law Review*, 2017, 80(6): 995–1025.

Frydman, B. J. *Le nouveau management de la justice et l'indépendence des juges*. Paris: Dalloz, 2011.

Jean, J.-P. P. *L'administration de la justice en Europe et l'évaluation de sa qualité*. Paris: Dalloz, 2005.

Katsh, E. and Rabinovich-Einy, O. *Digital Justice: Technology and the Internet of Disputes*, Oxford, Oxford University Press, 2017.

Kleinberg, J., Lakkaraju, H., Leskovec, J., Ludwig, J. and Mullainathan, S. "Human decisions and machine predictions", *The Quarterly Journal of Economics*, 2018, 133(1): 237–293, available at: https://doi.org/10.1093/qje/qjx032

Kosar, D. "Politics of judicial independence and judicial accountability in Czechia: Bargaining in the shadow of the law between court presidents and the Ministry of Justice", *European Constitutional Law Review*, 2017, 13(1): 96–123.

Lassègue, J. and Garapon, A. *Justice digitake: Révolution graphique et rupture anthropologie*, Paris: PUF, 2018.

Meniceur, Y. *L'intelligence artificielle en procès. Plaidoyer pour une réglementation internationale et européenne*. 1st édition Larcier, 2020.

Misa, T., Brey, P., and Feenberg, A. *Modernity and Technology*, Cambridge: MIT Press, 2003.

Morlino, L. *Equality, Freedom, and Democracy*, Oxford: Oxford University Press, 2020.

Morlino, L. and Sadurski, W. *Democratization and the European Union: Comparing Central and Eastern European Post-Communist Countries*, London, Routledge, 2010.

Piana, D. "Reforming the Judicary Through Standards", *International Review Administrative Science*, 2016, 1, 1–16.

Piana, D. "L'égalité comme enjeu dans les réformes de la justice", *La Revue Juridique Themis*, forthcoming.

Piana, D. and Verzelloni, L. "Quale governance della conoscenza nella giustizia digitale?" *Quaderni* di scienza politica, 2019, 26(3): 349–382.

Russell, S. and Norvig, P. *Artifical Intelligence: A Modern Approach*, Upper Saddle River: Prective Hall, 2009.

Stone Sweet, A. *Governing with Judges: Constitutional Politics in Europe*, Oxford: Oxford University Press, 2000.

Stone-Sweet, A. (2002), 'Judicialization and the Construction of Governance,' in M. Shapiro and A. Stone-Sweet (eds), *On Law, Politics, Judicialization*. Oxford: Oxford University Press.

Susskind, R. *Tomorrow's Lawyers: An Introduction to Your Future*, Oxford: Oxford University Press, 2013.

Tarissan, F. available at: https://afia.asso.fr/wp-content/uploads/2020/03/PSIA20-FabienTarissan.pdf, 2019.

Verzelloni, L. "Inside the Italian Law Firms", *SORTUZ*, 2017, 9: 25–45.

3   In search of fairness

A tale of ideal cities

The inspiration came from an unlikely encounter, one of those forms of serendipity that happens to you when you are in a context of research of multidisciplinary excellence and intersecting trajectories of artistic and intellectual linguistic growth that normally are not chosen, you simply find them unfolded in the lives of others. The story is animated by students and teachers. Among them, an inspiring teacher who worked with students with music and non verbal languages. He showed them their potential as designers of an ideal city. Not an individual exercise, rather a choral understanding of an ideal city. What are its rules? The architecture of its spaces, parks, accesses, roads, services? And, above all, what happens when that "ideal" city is born from the encounter of imaginations and experiences of very distant cities in terms of languages, cultures, rights and , in short, expectations and dreams.

We started with a challenge. Design your ideal cities, each on your own, each without consulting your neighbour. Draw. In silence. And that silence spoke. The look of Brazil on access to football, the gaze of China on the symmetry of the skyscrapers, the look of Mali on the water and the river, the look of Afghanistan on the interiors of homes (because without a home there is no ideal in any city in the world). And then forget about those paintings! Let's not talk about it at all. Compose a music that represents your (not mine, yours) city of ideal.

Three months, among a thousand things. What is an ideal city? After all, a place: it's not that we have to be all of us, but it could potentially be compatible with everyone's identity. And then you need rules, public spaces, parks, water and sports, and music and dance. It is not the return to the golden age. It is to get out of the silence that characterizes the foundations of our life together that are not explained, which we do not doubt because when we begin to doubt that it is already a problem, it is already a symptom of the loss of substantial legitimacy, the very assumptions of legality, the knowledge of the rules, the ability to manufacture the rules, to make them an object as abstract as it is, full of life.

On 17 May 2018, in an evening of moving public representation, 20 teenagers, with their roots in their lives and with their hands outstretched towards each other, sing "their" music, that of everyone, that of the ideal city, and the music says: "The hearts of men beats gently and slowly." Because we do not scream respect for the rules, we do it. This is the first form of legality that we would like to convey, that we would like to extend. Because after all, he was right, who in the world of philosophy, thinking of a hypothetical *experimentum crucis* on the rule of law (RoL), says: no society is so able to demonstrate the tightness of its rules as that which lives and makes the experience of difference.

Legality, primacy of the rule with respect to arbitrariness. Even before the sanction, even before the sentence, before any form of formal institutional intervention, respecting the primacy of the rules comes first. That legality that nobody talks about, but not because it does not need to be talked about, that is, it must be treated with natural language. It is simply consubstantial to our practice of living together, making the cognition of the quality of life a condition for strengthening the cognition of everybody living well.

All this does not imply ignoring the borders. It means starting from the citizens. In Brazil, in Mali, in China, in Afghanistan. At the end of the show, boys and girls were simply touched. Touched thanks to themselves and to the road they had made together. Such a great thing. The rhythm of music is a rule, dance is the experience of the rule. And all this was already in itself so much, so much to say. To their world, and to the world that will come.

The social dimension of legality

This chapter takes a different road from the one prospected in the international mainstream. The apparent detour will offer the reader an angle from which the picture sketched in Chapter 1 will get a more proportionate size and regain its own position in a broader – and more people-centred – perspective. The heuristic of the chapter is simple. Unsurprisingly, the amazing technological and computational advancements witnessed since the early 21st century create, without anyone willing to do so, an extraordinary opportunity to unpack the justice system and disentangle its building blocks. The exogenous factor – technology and data sciences – that are superficially denoted as neutral forces impinging upon a compact and cohesive system – the justice system – are, as a matter of fact and at a closer sight, rather the picklocks that enter the system from one of the several different doors – court management, legal reasoning, judicial drafting, digital forensics, and so on – and create a tunnel from which a fresh light casts a new rainbow of colors into the system. As if we were facing a daguerreotype, the abrupt arrival of 1) the computational rationality applied to a massive dataset and 2) the advanced digital tools throw a more penetrative and sharp light on what is comprised in the notion of justice, that is, the notion that we are used to take for granted both in terms of empirical and normative meanings.

More recently, the disruption of artificial intelligence as a promising horizon to renovate the justice system and improve the quality of the legal services supplied to citizens, enterprises and social groups, is in its own nature an unprecedented window that melts into a challenging and revealing process. By injecting massive computational rationality in a world made of natural language and dialectic rationality, the algorithms force all of us to go back to the foundations of the rule of law and to principles that lie at the basis of the legal and justice systems.

Let's go back to the tale of the ideal cities. The intense feeling offered by an open process of non-verbal dialogue that develops among young people whose notion of justice and legality is conceptually and linguistically framed in a wide range of different cultural settings – made of practices, experiences, concepts, images – represents a diagonal road towards a standing point where we are forced to seriously take up in our scientific and political agenda the question: what is the justice that people have in mind when they address the legal and justice institutions with their claims, their grievances and their demands? Despite sounding alien to the core business of those institutions that are engaged in the promotion of the quality of justice and the rule of law, the encounter between a system of justice that pivots on the principle of an autonomous impartial mechanism of adjudication and dispute settlement – the judge, whose independence is entrenched into the overall design of the rule of law institutions – and a system of problem solving that pivots on the principle of an objective, maximally efficient rationality, and a culturally neutral mechanism of calculus – artificial intelligence and digital devices that make its application possible – urges all of us to go back to the fundamentals.

What is the core of the rule of law? And to what extent may the computational rationality either strengthen or jeopardize the fairness of the response that legal services and justice institutions supply within a complex society?

Let's start by putting together the empirical puzzle. The responses collected and analysed through the 2012 European Social Survey pointed to a highly differentiated distribution of citizens' attitudes towards justice institutions. The sample of countries must be considered in terms of representativeness only with reference to the European space. This notwithstanding, people seem to address different demands to the legal and justice institutions, which range from greater impartiality to more effectiveness. According to the European Social Survey – module focusing on justice – if asked to reply to the question whether laws may be sometimes considered as unfair to the point of justifying a law breach, Belgium, Switzerland, Denmark, Estonia, France, Netherlands, Norway, Sweden and Slovenia feature a dominant majority of positive answers, which are inversely distributed in Bulgaria, Czech Republic, Spain, Croatia, Greece, and Cyprus.

If assessed against an homogenous sample of countries, which have in common both the legal framework of the EC law and an overall tradition of established rule of law, the findings cast new light on the perception of the judicial independence citizens have within the European Union and add further evidence that reinforces the thesis that consists in claiming a deeply differential pattern of trust in the legal and justice systems within the European Union.

Countries notably differ both in the magnitude of distrust and in the overall trends of deepening or worsening the perception of independence. Beside countries that feature a high degree of continuity – such as Denmark, Finland, Austria – coupled with an irregular degree of perceived independence – much higher in Denmark than the other two countries – we observe countries with a continuity on the negative direction, such as Poland, the Czech Republic, and countries that show significant improvement – such as France, Spain, and Italy. This empirical evidence must be assessed once framed in the context of the overall supply of legal services and justice responses that each country has set up. Countries that have adopted new tools to facilitate the adoption of extra-judicial mechanisms of dispute settlement – the far largest majority – did not experience a proportionate and consequential decrease of the incoming litigious cases, especially in the field of civil and commercial law. In some specific contexts, people seem to prefer a lawsuit in order to end up with a final adjudication made by a judge, something that also happens in countries where the judicial independence is perceived as only partially de facto assured. This is the case for instance in all Southern European countries. Equally uneven in terms of trust is the strategy of promoting transparency and accessibility of judicial judgments, which is one of the key common trends in the European Union today (DG Justice European Commission 2020).

The data we have today at the disposal of policy makers and stakeholders in the field of the quality of justice cast a dark light on the genuine nature of the correlation between efficiency and accessibility, both strengthened by digital transformation and the quality of justice experienced by citizens. By claiming the "non-genuine" linearity, the working hypothesis may shift to a more nuanced and articulated notion of demand of justice, rather than to a radical rejection of the extraordinary – and obviously positive – potential of the scientific and technological advancements.

To formulate the question in a more responsive and empirically adequate manner, the findings of the World Justice Project about the pathfinders and the barriers witnessed by laypeople in the world when they need to find a legal solution to their social and economic problems are very telling. Data collected through the World Justice Project 2019 focused specifically on the gaps and the barriers people meet when they try to find lawful solutions to their problems, or when they claim for rights enforcement or sanctions for violation, and they have been collected by means of a legal needs survey tool elaborated in the framework of the Agenda 2030 – OECD Justice Initiative. OECD Initiative on Access to Justice (and related actions, such as legal needs surveying and actions aiming at achieving the SDG 16 Goals).[1]

Findings are quite revealing about the extent of the justice gap people experience across the globe:

> 1.5 billion people cannot obtain justice for civil, administrative or criminal justice problems. These are victims of crime and people with civil and administrative justice needs who may live in contexts with functioning institutions and justice systems, but who face obstacles to solve their everyday justice issues … 4.5 billion people are excluded from the opportunities provided by law.
> (https://worldjusticeproject.org/our-work/research-and-data/
> access-justice/measuring-justice-gap)

These are people who lack legal tools – including identity documents, land or housing tenure, and formal work arrangements – that allow them to protect their assets and access the economic opportunities or public services to which they are entitled (World Justice Project 2019).

Furthermore, countries differ in the type of justice gap experienced by residents: civil and criminal justice systems often do not have the same pattern of qualities and facilitating conditions to ensure that the demands of justice receive the right answer and, even if this may be the case, the enforcement mechanisms that are put into motion vary from

1 https://www.oecd.org/gov/access-to-justice.htm

one type of proceeding to the other, giving overall an uneven spectrum of legal services and institutional capacities to guarantee justice for all.

The main consequences are of two types: a) people experience different types of problems and develop different types of demands to the potential improvements that may derive from the introduction of technologies and computational devices supporting and strengthening the delivering capacity of legal and justice institutions; b) countries that have adopted, under the influence of a comprehensive strategy of quality of justice promotion, similar tools and similar policies to "go digital" – as in the case of the member states of the Council of Europe – do not feature similar trends in the responses citizens believe they may get if they have to lodge a complaint in the justice sector.

This differential pattern on the side of the expectations of people who live in different countries and who face different demands of justice goes hand in hand with the differential impact that the policies adopted to promote a more effective and a more efficient justice brought about. For instance, the European member States, old and new ones, underwent the waves of judicial reforms, under the soft and gentle influence of these new modes of governance, set up by judicial networks and horizontal learning mechanisms. However, if the data are taken seriously, there is no considerable difference in the assessment of the rule of law that comes out from the worldwide round of governance assessment (such as the one set up by the World Bank for three decades). Despite the similar approach that underlies the range of reforms adopted in those European countries that gave a strong managerial impulse to judicial reforms through the digital technologies, the outcome achieved in terms of rule of law is very variegated from country to country. This is only to say that despite the same internationally shaped and globally standardized promise of better justice through the digital medium, people living in countries that have actually experienced the digital turn show 1) a different distribution of expectations for the fairness of the system and 2) a different distribution of experiences about the efficiency of the system.

Qualities of justice people want

Setting up, maintaining, and making perennial a highly responsive, truly effective, and actually trustworthy system of legal services and justice responses seems to be, unquestionably, a major challenge for most of the countries in the world. Also, those countries that are ranked first in terms of efficiency and managerial quality do face the challenge to ensure the continuity and predictability of the functioning of the legal services' providers and the justice institutions. Instead, in countries that feature a low degree of quality in terms of perceived independence and efficiency, the key trade-off to be made consists in balancing equal access to all against an effective response to all needs and problems.

In the repertoire of notions and conceptual tools elaborated by the international actors engaged in the promotion of the quality of justice, something still seems to remain largely underexplored. Where does the demand of legal services and justice responses come from? What are the building blocks of the "demand"? Why, despite the increased visibility and transparency, is the reaction of people not linearly positive? This paragraph digs into this puzzle.

What we have learnt from a vast array of researches conducted in the field of the law and society, as well as in the field of law and economics, is that more timely and predictable judicial decisions are of utmost importance in facilitating entrance and exit from the markets, managing capital flowing and human resources development, as well as ensuring financial entrepreneurship and investing planning. The scholarship is well established on this point and it has reached a sophistication in the analysis that goes as far as measuring the potential impact of legal uncertainty in fields such as public procurement, international trade, and economic growth. We also know, on the basis of an established literature, that a de jure impartial judiciary impacts deeply and widely on the stability of societies and on their capacity to feed long-term development strategies.

And yet, we know that the correlations established between macro variables do not offer an exhaustive picture of the engine that works at the heart of the system that we can call "law-society-economy". Far from being linear, the causality featured by this system goes in a double sense to connect the law to social development and, vice versa, the social dimensions to the enforcement of the laws.

The relevance of the social dimensions for the quality of justice can be pointed out by considering a first, crucial variable, which is trust. Which trust? Trust whom and in which institution? And at what level should it be measured?

As already said, the balance between judicial independence and judicial accountability seems to be lacking in touching all the engines responsible for the overall quality of the judicial function, both in the way it operates and in the type of deliverables that it offers citizens. This points to the existence of a third – and still missing – dimension. *To detect this dimension, an epistemological shift is needed. In fact, in the rule of law and quality of justice promotion the "law and justice" phenomenon is mostly related to the functioning of the courts.* A potential insight to make this shift may come from the sociology of law and from the analysis of institutions. In the rich scholarship developed on the law-society relationship and on the society-politics relationship it is possible to obtain fruitful insights. Scholars have insistently stressed the importance of culture, social capital and civic sense as favourable conditions for well-functioning institutions.

The sociology of law has also widely investigated the demand of justice and the perception of the law. Reviewing this literature is almost impossible in this limited space. We can however refer to the recent Commaille (2015, pp. 369ss), for a critical appraisal and an insightful proposal on this topic. The point we want to underline is that the four streams – rule of law promotion, quality of justice, sociology of law, and political analysis of the institutions – have never entered into a multi-disciplinary dialogue. This seriously undermines not only our analytical capacity to understanding a complex and crucial phenomenon as "law and justice" but, at the same time, it jeopardizes the capacity of policy makers to design effective and responsive policies in the judicial sector.

Trust appears as the missing link between institutional and organizational reforms and the rule of law. Trust is a subject that has long been covered by a vast and variegated scholarship in the social and political sciences. The key point here for the scope of this work is which trust? Trust what? The seminal work of Charles Tilly, *Trust and Rules*, offers a hint here. It seems to pave the way towards a promising hypothesis. The rule of law is, as a matter of fact, a specific setting in which impersonal rules have primacy. This primacy is entrenched in the legal codes and constitutional provisions as much as they are embedded in the checks and balances featured by the institutions. However, the primacy of the rule should somehow be embedded in the culture of the ruled. A society whose citizens do not endorse, as a Kantian principle, the idea that rules should hold super parties and should be impersonal and impartially applied is a society where the rule of law, even supported by strong and strict mechanisms of enforcement, will easily fall victim to the resilience of diffuse culture (Tyler 2003). If this is so, the first important consequence is that the trust we need in a stable rule of law is the generic trust, a trust in the anonymous other. The trustful feelings experienced for the members of close networks are not the kind of feelings we need for the primacy of the impersonal rule, that is, the necessary condition for the rule of law. How do we connect this reasoning to courts?

Trust in courts looks more like a durable outcome of a respectful rule of law system, rather than being a founding component of it. It seems that we are at an impasse. Sociology of law might be helpful in this respect. Going back to its origin, the founding father of sociology argued that the texture of a society is a key component of its normative order. One can inject the most sophisticated set of rules into a socio-political system without achieving any durable result if people do not respect them. This is, however, still a trivial and surface statement. The deepest root of the rule of law is in the belief in the value of reciprocity. This is to argue that the founding determinant of the RoL is not legal in its nature, it is pre-legal. Scholars have already touched on this point. In societies where a high respect for the social order is internalized, the need for an external, authoritative intervention in order to make this order protected, maintained and durable is less requested. Therefore, the agenda of judicial institutions is inevitably smaller. A low degree of litigation has a reflex in a high level of RoL in those contexts where conflicts are settled on the basis of a high degree of civicness (Rothstein 2011). By focusing on the pre-legal dimension of the rule of law, a scholar may be accused of naïve optimism. If, on the one hand, the rule of law proves to be a vague concept, on the other hand, pre-legal aspects show obstinacy to the empirical investigation. Indeed, their exploration is forced to deal with an endless puzzle of social scientists, that is, the untouchable nature of not observable forces, whose effects we can measure and whose intrinsic ontology we can just guess (Boudon 1984). However, by denying the importance of pre-legal aspects of rule of law one does not get very far in either understanding the very way society functions or in providing policy makers with sound frameworks to set their agenda in legal and judicial reforms (Piana 2010). A way out would be to extend the meaning of the notion of the rule of law concept to incorporate those aspects that directly refer to pre-legal dimensions of social enterprises. In this way, the rule of law would simply mean the primacy of rules, whereas the determinacy of what these rules are, where they come from and where they are going, remains an open question to be addressed empirically.

As a matter of fact, rules used in a society to deal with an inescapable part of social life – disagreement (Besson 2005) – might have different sources and different formats. The analytical strategy to adopt here is the following. The outbreak of the digital transformation and the sudden acceleration it is experiencing, across nations and cultures, must be seen as a call for a higher awareness and a more open and inclusive debate as how (and on which political and social ground) the proportions among different principles, values, and social desiderata are part of the the the design of every technological and scientific artefact. Rule of law deprived of a substratum from which it draws its own legitimacy may become an arid terrain, the lymph of a perfectly designed legal mechanism, but emptied of a cultural soul. In this respect, entrenching the fundamental rights in nascent democracies does not seem to address proficiently the urgent question of where the rule of law gets its substantial legitimacy. The charters of fundamental rights are, after all, artificial creations of legal and political elites, which may encounter the legitimacy of citizens – but this legitimacy will always come ex post. In general, these contributions draw attention to the political-institutional dimension of the *rule of law*. In a different way, Russell Hardin (Hardin 1993, p. 98) interprets the *rule of law* as a rule of rules *spontaneously* born to solve problems of social coordination where conditions of pluralism of values and preferences exist. According to Hardin the concept of rule of law denotes those systems of collective action in which power asymmetry exists. He thus puts emphasis on the importance of the social fabric that underlies the functioning of institutions. Rule of law cultural dimensions are pivotal. Communities where disagreements and conflicts are faced by means of specific strategies of muddling through, revenges, eventually violence, or simply indifference, do not appear to be promising fields in which the rule of law can be firmly established and rooted. Only where law is considered a fair and legitimate instrument to deal with conflicts is the rule of law respected as leading principle inspiring human behaviours. Therefore, the rule of law may be thought of as a social system in which interactions, both social and political, are ruled and shaped according to impartial, stable, and predictable fundamental rules, some of them of *longue durée*.

The perspective suggested by scholars when the social dimensions of the rule of law are considered as facilitating conditions to the consolidation and the institutionalization of impartial and impersonal mechanisms of dispute settlement opens, by the same token, an interesting perspective on the role played by trust and trustworthiness in ensuring that people, despite their different ideas about a "good society", their different interests, their different preferences, their differences values, behave in accordance with the overarching principle that is summarized by the idea of the primacy of the rule.

Trust is, in this respect, a dimension of the social dimension of legality. Trust is a cognitive disposition, at the individual level, and a feature of a system. At the individual level trust is better understood from the point of view of "street-level epistemology", that is, how people build their beliefs and how they rely on these beliefs. In some cases, trust and acceptance of a set of beliefs are both seen as reasonable attitudes, whereas distrust comes out as too costly, challenging, or demanding in terms of information, expertise, skills, competences (Hardin 1993).

Trust and normative compliance emerge from the recursive played type of game, played in social contexts where actors have experienced that the other's behaviour takes place according to a set of common rules. This is to say that the social conditions that influence the pattern of interaction linking up law with society are intimately interlaced with the contexts in which people "play". Susan Silbey was right by pointing out the deeply context-sensitive common sense of the law, something that generally applies to the common sense of all types of norms. Trust and common sense of the law are of utmost importance in understanding what it means in a society, under specific historical conditions and in a given historical time frame, to demand a lawful response to conflicts, grievances, claims, and violations of rights that people experience. In fact, people do not experience judicial facts: first they experience social problems, economic dilemmas, psychological traumas, and they turn to the legal system to receive an answer.

Now it is the time to dig into the nature of the expected answer: what kind of justice are laypeople and social groups looking for? Is there a difference between the answer that small and medium-sized enterprises want from the legal and justice sector and the answer that international corporations are inclined to seek? There is. Qualifying the demand of justice and entering the very nature of the expected answer that different actors in society are demanding from the legal and justice sector means taking seriously the vast range of services and solutions that are today produced in the legal market and understanding that the complex matrix of legal and judicial responses cover a much larger spectrum than what is handled and governed under the traditional setting of judicial governance. Courts are just part of a wider system of paths and pathfinding facilitators, mechanisms of allocation of values and resources, which include, but in an exclusive manner, adjudication.

According to the sociological evidence we have at our disposal today, we know that the reason people have to claim depends on a tetragon of factors.

First, the different distribution of trust to the institutions influences the choice people make when they seek a solution to what they experience as vital problems: divorces, family conflicts, property rights recognition, grievances rising in the workplace, consumer rights violation, commercial duties that are not respected, just to list some examples that instantiate what happens in daily life. Where to go when such a problem occurs? Where to find a solution? The answers to this first dilemma, which is instrumental to the research of the subsequent steps and stages in the settlement of a potential dispute, may be found in informal and formal terms, within informal institutions – such as social relationships, acquaintances – or within formal institutions – professional associations, trade unions, interest representative institutions and courts. By making this first choice, trust plays a generic and a specific function about the formulation of expectations: in addition to the more generic trust in the legal and justice system, trust in the professionalism of the sources of information matters enormously in terms of where to go and which information has to be deemed as reliable and sound. Furthermore, laypeople may also decide not to seek legal solutions within the formal institutions and rather to turn to lawful and still informal solutions, such as those that can be achieved with mutual agreement, negotiation and social normativity in general.

These remarks are here made to recall the importance of the social and cultural context where each type of digital device introduced in the interface people/justice, and more general as a facilitator in the pathfinding strategy of laypeople to reach a solution for their problems must be considered and assessed "in context". Here the word context has a very compounded meaning, ranging from trust to the expected reliability of the vast offer of normativity that a society has at its disposal, largely embedded in the silent and tacit social knowledge integrated into the daily practices of social interactions. For instance, in societies where people repeatedly violate social norms, social trust is eroded to the point that people feel uncertain in some social interactions. In a sense, stable and durable social trust is a good indicator of internalized social norms.

Furthermore, trust is fed by civic engagement. Not a generic commitment, but the engagement in the design of those policies which they consider as more critical and more valuable for their social life. Here comes civil engagement in the design of judicial reforms and in the design of user-oriented policy tools. In fact, trust is directly affected by the predictability of the trial timeframe and the potential costs of the proceedings. The stability of civil and criminal procedures as well as the stability and reliability of the rule enforcement mechanisms are critical preconditions of trust. Trust is also directly affected by the intelligibility of the proceedings and the procedures. Nobody trusts a game if she or he does not understand the rules. Therefore, the accessibility of legal language is a key component, even if it does not exhaust the entire spectrum of the building blocks of the demand for a reliable, intelligible, and potentially extensible response to an infinite number of others in the same situation. Deference of the Kantian principle does not stand as an absolute, however. Laypeople who experience severe economic or social problems related to structural conditions of inequalities may want to have access to tailor-made legal services to respond to their needs. More generally it the query for a responsive and socially significant AI can not be avoided by means of a 'by design' solution. Crafting artefacts is not a way to regain the certainty and the objectivity of a rational (and Cartesian) method applied into capital sectors of the social life, such as health, mobility, energy. Here add the reference to Hubert et Stuart Dreyfus, From Socrates to Expert Systems: The Limits and Dangers of Calculative Rationality, 2004 e Christian Byk, Le droit et l'idée de perfectibilité humaine, Revue de la recherche juridique, PUAM, 2017-4, pp.1379–1408.

The idea is that the delivering capacity of judicial institutions, including the capacity to deal with different stakeholders, is a key ingredient of trust. The starting point should be carefully and deeply assessed in order to set up the most adequate strategies, given the actual conditions in which societies and citizens are living. Abstract-designed models might be very misleading if they are not implemented with a context-oriented approach.

Reasons to trust[2]

The upheaval of digital technologies that first penetrate our daily life and afterwards deeply and widely transformed our economies and our political institutions is not a simple exogenous shock that impinges upon social systems, triggering new ways of doing things and new forms of interactions, competitions, collaborations, and interdependences. Rather, the very nature of the digital transformation is of the kind of institutional facts, those which are irrigated by embedded normativity and that consequently get an overall significance beyond the immediate and punctual advantages they may bring to one or the other actor. Surely, the digital turn has made possible new winners and new losers and has thereby entailed a massive and unpredictable redistribution of stakes and stakeholders all over the globe. However, the most disruptive and compelling impact of it consists in questioning at the most foundational level the contract that lies at the base of our societies. This contract is made up of expected behaviours respectful of the rules, procedures for the distribution, allocation, and reallocation of authoritative power, and the cutting-edge between duties and rights. This contract consists of an explicit part – which is entrenched in the rules of the social and political game – and an implicit (or tacit) part – which is embedded in the way "social institutions think" (Douglas 1986).

Despite the importance and the role acknowledged to formal rules and explicit constraints, the cognitive/cultural dimensions of the social institutions play an equally – if not stronger – role in determining the stability and the continuity of the rule of law. A different way to see this point may come from the following consideration: societies are tied by implicit social contracts that stand at the basis of the interplay between social groups. The beliefs they endorse about the actual enforcement of the social rules and the expectations social actors do have as to the behaviours of the others – whether compliant with the rules or not – are crucial in the empirical understanding of the interaction law and society unfold "in context" – cultural and historical contexts:

---

2 This paragraph draws from the official documents adopted by the OECD and the OECD OSII partnership. The OECD stream on access to justice and the documents portraying the principles, strategies, criteria, and framework dimensions are available at www.oecd.org/gov/access-to-justice.htm

A culture of lawfulness means that the population in general follows the law and has a desire to access the justice system to address their grievances. It does not require that every single individual in that society believe in the feasibility or even the desirability of the rule of law but that the average person believes that formal laws are a fundamental part of justice or can be used to attain justice and that the justice system can enhance his or her life and society in general.

(Godson 2000)

The strength of the social contract also lies in its tacit nature. People do not refer to it until the moment it is questioned. Yet, the tacit expectations of laypeople when they address their claims to justice systems are of vital importance for its legitimacy: "the judge spends some of his time listening to me", explains a person waiting for the hearing in the corridor of a courthouse. Two key words must be taken for further consideration: "listening" and "time".

Beyond the legal determinants that have been mostly addressed by ambitious institutional programs, with the aim of establishing formal guarantees of equality, dignity; fair treatment in case of conflicts and disputes, notably in those circumstances that are related to the interactions individuals may have with the bench, the rule of law is unquestionably tied up to the attitudes individuals adopt to deal with social diversities, rule-oriented behaviours, and rule-based judgments of others' behaviour, as well as economic strategies to achieve better living conditions for themselves and their acquaintances and relatives.

Little surprise that this view is the consensus of the majority. Intuitively we all understand that it would be hard to rule a system under conditions of fairness and equality if these same concepts do not correspond to the principles that shape and guide the daily actions of individuals. It would be a chimera, a system based on the rule of law in which actors prefer to violate the rules and the maintenance of the order is generally ensured by sanctioning and punitive strategies.

Yet once consensus has been reached on these general and uncontestable points of view, much more controversial remains the path we should choose to entrench these principles in the policies set up by the institutions to educate children and young people in the rule of law and to create favorable conditions along the entire lifelong learning process of adults who face almost every day innovations, risks, uncertainty, conflicts, differences, and yet are still expected to handle all these challenges on the basis of a conduct inspired by the principle of the rule of law. This becomes even more crucial and vital in the case of individuals who serve as public officers or as judges/prosecutors/high-ranking functionaries in the rule of law institutions, such as the police, the home affairs offices, custom offices, migration departments, and so on.

Digital technologies and computational rationalities applied to the legal and justice sector are, to some extent, the basis of a new social contract. They promise to eradicate both arbitrariness and inefficiency, the most severe bugs that jeopardize the trust people are ready to grant to legal and justice institutions.

To go back to our initial point, whether the social conditions may facilitate, encourage, or oppose the use of ICT and digital devices within the justice system, it seems that the qualities of justice that citizens experience as not satisfying may be a potential target for the introduction of comprehensive innovations pivoting around digital technology and the potential of information science. As a matter of fact, remote answers, automated solutions, and digitalized devices through which the range of previous responses may be made available to the broad public so that it is possible (also for someone who has no specialized legal expertise) to assess autonomously whether to seek the solution in the spectrum of possible responses that may come from the legal and justice sector create a promising viaticum to fill the gap between the demand and the offer of legal services and justice responses. And still, this is not so linear and patently granted as it may seem at a first analysis. If the reasoning moves away from a superficial and purely efficiency-oriented approach, it will encounter other dimensions, such as the nature of the demands that come from laypeople and economic actors. Some of them are seeking the recognition of their identity as rights-holders. In social contexts where social trust is eroded by a long history of conflict and society did not manage to create solid and safe networks for the production and distribution of services, the search for a third impartial mechanism to settle the disputes that arise in the context of economic transactions and social interactions seems to become vital in the way the encounter between people and the legal and justice sector is assured. In this interplay, the intervention of the automation, as effective and efficient it may be, would not add a more responsive service to people's needs. However, one must not be blind to or neglect the potential that technologies do bring in terms of filling gaps and dismantling barriers.

The point to underline here is that, among the range of parameters that must be put together to compose the new compass that legal and justice institutions need when affected by the digital turn, one should refer directly to the importance of those normative dimensions that are embedded in the "culture" of a society and even more significantly within the "culture" of the communities and the social groups.

It is to be expected that social and political contexts that experience deterioration in the trust people have in courts with the introduction of automated devices to take decisions in the field of justice administration is more widely and easily accepted than in systems where courts enjoy a high degree of trust. To phrase the question that citizens may be ready to ask in simple terms: better a judge or a robot? If the perception of arbitrariness and opacity is diffuse, the answer to the question may be surprisingly oscillating towards the second option. But if this is the case, the new compass to govern these new phenomena must include specific mechanisms that ensure that cultural dimensions are taken into consideration and that the only recipe that fits all approaches is abandoned.

Cultural dimensions are not living "outside": it is not an exogenous factor impinging upon individual thoughts and actions. Laypeople are a lively culture and culture moves with them on their legs and hands, crossing borders and shaking established and taken-for-granted destinies. Culture is at the same time a resource that individuals shape, reshape, handle, and refer to as the result of their social interactions, memories, representations, and institutions. A legitimate, reliable, and accountable pattern of an interactional citizens-justice system is a goal for all forms of social and economic development. However, in the culture of lawfulness we have found several aspects that deserve our careful and skillful consideration. Problem-solving situations in which people need to mobilize their dispositions to find a solution that is perceived as legitimate rather than arbitrary by others already feature important facets of the search for a rule which responds to the principle of the rule primacy. The law, in this respect, is a rule that is enforced through the justice system but is rooted in the culture of lawfulness. This latter is made of the social representations and practices that are pivoting on impersonal mechanism of dispute resolution.

Influencing the chain of trust and expectations that link people to legal and justice institutions, digital technology, and computations reshuffle the social contract: the myth of a society based on a responsible agency, embedded in legal and judicial institutions, whose conflicts had to be settled by impersonal – but still human – mechanisms and whose ultimate deliberative arena compensates and balances different values and principles under the absolute primacy of the law. Robots and automated agents did not belong to the picture painted in this myth.

The practical added value of these remarks to the current mainstream is threefold:

- Justice systems are not only considered as court-based system, but complex systems in which courts do play unquestionably a pivotal role, but not exclusively. Non-judicial or extra-judicial methods of dispute settlement are equally important as judicial ones. Mechanisms of triage, legal education, legal empowerment, legal services, and clinics participate in the complex matrix of the justice system, as well as the courts.

- Citizens regain the centre of the political discourse. A wide range of policy instruments introducing monitoring tools is available. They are mostly managed from an organizational perspective: the efficiency of the courts system is, in a way, an instance of this general approach which pivots on the idea of the efficiency of the input/output ratio. The roundtable discussion fully took stock of the results of these exercises, both in terms of methods and content, but moved on by opening up a new perspective, which was citizen-based. Citizens (and companies) turn to justice systems and demand from them answers and services. They address litigious instances and get back solutions and settlements. For this reason, equality is meant as equality of opportunities, "equality of access".

- Equality: the roundtables debated a lot about equality as a richer concept than the one used in legal discourse, as equality before the law. Beside this, which remains a necessary condition for the rule of law, the equality considered refers rather to chances, opportunities. The idea here is that the slower, more opaque and unresponsive the justice system is about the demands of justice that society addresses to the "law in action", the more it can perpetuate or eventually worsen economic, social, and cultural inequalities.

By mentioning the different economic and social conditions in which people seek legal service or a response from the justice system, one engages in the analysis of the relationships that connect legal needs to other social, economic, and cultural dimensions of citizens' lives. In this respect, by targeting the inequalities that jeopardize equal access to justice, the inspiring hypothesis consists in saying that a more responsive, citizen-centred justice system can break established patterns of inequalities, which might worsen if access to justice is not equally possible for all. Equal access should be ensured to different groups of people or citizens who have different capacities and resources. Therefore, scouting the capacities, surveying the needs, mapping the demands and monitoring the effects of access to justice policies are all crucial to ensure that justice systems contribute significantly to make inclusive and durable growth and human development. Access to justice may feature specific or generic barriers, which turn out to be costs for individuals and socioeconomic actors (including business actors) to

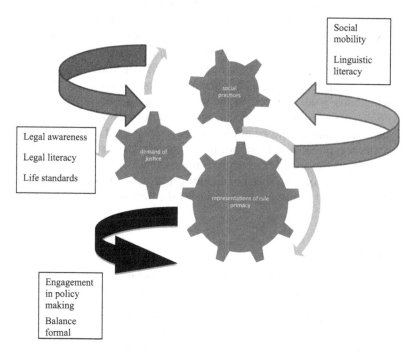

Figure 3.1 Synopsis of the dimensions of the social dimension of legality

solve their legal problems. This holds even more for those actors who belong to disadvantaged groups such as individuals with mental illness, the unemployed, poorly educated people, and so on. Therefore, barriers in accessing legal services – and consequently, to the solutions to legal problems – have the effect of initial costs for the individuals and multiplying inequalities (for disadvantaged citizens).

Here a distinction must be made: access to justice comes as a second step in a much broader and comprehensive process which starts with access to the ensemble of the legal norms. In this respect, the notion of access is translated into the notion of understanding and figuring out how to rely upon the legal system to reach a solution for the problems they have. The link between the intelligible pathways to justice and trust in the justice system becomes more evident and clearer if the above remark is taken into consideration. The empirical research conducted in comparative terms about the generic trust that people are inclined to award to the justice system show that it is also related to the stability of the system itself and to the intelligibility of its rules, procedural and substantial. Only under conditions of stability and intelligibility is it possible, eventually, to avoid the expectations of arbitrariness that lay-people may feel once they interact with a complex set of norms and procedures whose rationale they do not understand. Intelligibility is not only dependent on the language used in legal drafting and institutional communications, as important both of these aspects may be. Intelligibility is also related to the existence of significant rituals and symbols, which echo in the social representations of what is a justice system and what should be a fair justice system: "trust depends on the way the social reality is built, not in the constructivist sense, but in the sense of how the reliable and stable is the existence of social and institutional tools performing specific functions" (Berger and Luckman 1966).

Let's go back, once again, to people: the new compass must pivot around them.

References

Berger, P. L. and Luckman, T. *The Social Construction of Reality: A Treatise in the Sociology of Knowledge*, New York: Anchor Books, 1966.

Besson, S. *The Morality of Conflict: Reasonable Disagreement and the Law*, Bloomsbury Publishing, Hart Publishing, London, 2005.

Boudon, R. *La place du désourdre*, Paris: PuF, 1984.

Commaille, J. *A Quoi Nous Sert le Droit?* Paris: Gallimard, 2015

Douglas, M. *How Institutions Think*. Syracuse: Syracuse University Press, 1986.

European Justice Scoreboard, DG Justice European Commission, 2020, available at: https://ec.europa.eu/commission/presscorner/detail/en/IP_20_1316

Godson, R. "A Guide to Developing a Culture of Lawfulness" presented at the Symposium on the Role of Civil Society in Countering Organized Crime: Global Implications of the Palermo, Sicily Renaissance, 2000.

Hardin, R. "The street-level epistemology of trust", *Politics & Society*, 1993, 21(4): 505–529.

Piana, D. *Judicial accountabilities in new Europe*, Aldershot: Ashgate, 2010.

Rothstein, B. *The Quality of Government: Corruption, Social Trust and Inequality in International Perspective*, Chicago: University of Chicago Press, 2011.

Tyler, Tom R. "Procedural justice, legitimacy, and the effective rule of law." *Crime and Justice*, 2003, 30: 283–357.

World Justice Project, available at: https://worldjusticeproject.org/our-work/research-and-data/access-justice/measuring-justice-gap, 2019.

4 System of intelligences

Stories we presumably shall read

In Mr Palomar's life there was a period when his rule was this: first, to construct in his mind a model, the most perfect, logical, geometrical model possible; second, to see if the model was suited to the practical situations observed in experiences; third, to make the corrections necessary for model and reality to coincide ... a model is by definition that in which nothing has to be changed. ... a delicate work of adjustment was then required. In other words if the model does not succeed in transforming reality, reality must succeed in transforming the model ... but the model becomes a kind of fortress whose thick walls conceal what is outside. Mr Palomar, who from powers and counter-powers expects always the worst, was finally convinced that what really counts is what happens despite them: the form that the society is assuming slowing, silently, anonymously, in people's habits, their ways of thinking and acting, their scales of values.

(Calvino 1986 (tr. engl.))

The factor within the engine of a complex system

The genius of Calvino is still provocative and timely in recalling for us the unavoidable gap that separates models from reality. Despite the quest for models and standards that mark the entire range of strategies and policies deployed since the 1970s to promote the rule of law and afterward the quality of justice, reality escapes and offers steadily and persistently good reasons to go back to models, revise them, or simply overcome them. Despite several different conceptions of the rule of law that have been endorsed within these policies (Piana 2010; Ginsburg 2009), the programs and projects financed by the World Bank, the Council of Europe, the European Commission, USAID, and many other actors, all converge on the pivotal role played by the procedural dimension of the rule of law, the impact that the legal system may have on the institutional stability and the social prosperity, by the entrenchment of constitutional or statutory laws of the guarantees of judicial independence (Dallara and Piana 2015). In Europe this has gone hand in hand with the promotion of a self/governing court system (Council of Europe, CCJE 2007) where a high judicial council, composed of a majority of magistrates elected by peers, is responsible for the recruitment, the promotion, and the evaluation of judges. Despite the ever-growing effort put on the "working site" which is represented by the promotion of the rule of law via the promotion of institutional guarantees of judicial independence and of the guarantees of fair trial, the relationship between the improvement of the rule of law and the introduction of the high court judgment (HCJ) is anything but linear. In recent work it has been shown that the rule of law and judicial independence are interlaced by a strong and complex relationship (Vigour 2018). Scholars argued that, even if judicial independence is a necessary condition for the rule of law, it is far from being sufficient to determine the rule of law. Answering the question "which further conditions are playing a role?" has become compelling.

In a way, the quality of justice policy stream aims to provide an answer to this question: "how the actual functioning of the justice system ensures that rights are enforced and the demands of justice are met and fully answered?". This happens by adding the notion of quality to the notion of the rule of law. If, traditionally, compliance to the rule of law was deemed as a necessary and sufficient condition to ensure that legal needs and demands of justice were met, today, with the shift to the quality of justice paradigm, the responsiveness to a set of different and connected criteria, among which the rule of law, is considered as the guarantee of a system that deliver justice. These criteria include the answerability of the justice system, the access to the remedies to the violations of rights, and the accountability from the managerial and the communicational point of view. It does not mean that the rule of law is denied. It is rather the opposite. Compliance with those criteria that point to a well-functioning system is considered as a way to strengthen the rule of law. Scholars and practitioners have referred to the quality of justice since the early 1990s. This has come together with the growing interest devoted to court management, managerial and public accountability as they are applied to the judicial sector (Jean 2005; Pauliat 2007; Piana 2009). The reasoning behind this new policy stream is very simple. A fair trial is not only expected to be respectful of the procedural codes and fundamental rights, but it should also comply with the standard of a reasonable timeframe. Moreover, it is desirable that a judicial institution is not only independent, but also transparent and predictable in terms of results and resource management. This leads to the introduction of a conception of quality of justice that goes beyond the principle of the rule of law, while still incorporating it. This approach has become streamlined in the EU. For more than two decades, a vast repertoire of instruments, such as checklists, recommendations, monitoring and assessment tools, benchmarks, and so on, have been developed and subsequently become widespread across the countries that adhere to the European institutions, such as the European Union and the Council of Europe.

Yet still the gap between, on the one hand, the demand addressed by citizens and stakeholders to the justice systems and, on the other hand, the answer provided by the domestic justice systems as well as the supranational judicial institutions seems to be stretched by several intervening variables: the increasing (and ever growing) demand for rights enforcement; the uneven litigation rate level; the reactivity of the social and economic disputes to market fluctuation and credit/ monetary instability; the transformation of street criminality; the widespread influence of the administrative jurisdictions, notably in dispute settlement concerning public procurement cases and in general public service providers' litigations.

Under these complex conditions the quality of justice that is necessary to ensure both input and output legitimacy called, once again, for a comprehensive assessment and revision. After the shift from a paradigm of rule of law promotion, which was centred on the formal guarantees of judicial impartiality, to a paradigm of organizational and managerial quality of justice centred on the substantial performance of the court systems, the international debate moved forward and enriched the quality of justice paradigm to include a further dimension, which is represented by equal access to justice (OCDE 2019).

Having these standards as a background – rule of law, quality of justice, and equal access to justice – which put an emphasis on different dimensions of a unique, comprehensive, and complex system – the justice system – the multiple waves of technological innovations and computational applications to the legal and justice sector unveiled the role played by a further dimension: intelligence.

Intelligence is a tricky concept whose core dimension is far from being neutral. As all concepts that keep a deep and strong link to the anthropomorphic vision of processes and phenomena, intelligence is something that we say of one reaction that is good, which is worth imitating because of its capacity to solve problems. The fundamental human dimension of the intelligence as a notion comes out with more evidence once we consider the kind of intelligence that is not human, notably artificial intelligence. This is a method to solve a problem that, to some extent, emulates the manners to solve problems that human beings tend to adopt without, by the same token, falling victim to the traps and mistakes that human beings are unable to avoid. The failing nature of human intelligence is here meant in terms of computational potential.

Some questions that arise are: which intelligences are embedded into the justice systems? Who are those actors that are holders of these intelligences? How are these intelligences transferred and recognized? To what extent does the turn-over of actors touch upon the embedded intelligences kept alive by the functioning of the system?

To reply, on the basis of the empirical evidence we have at our disposal, means in a way to abandon models and one-size-fits-all recipes. By the same token, we will gain, as an exchange, a better understanding of the interplay between the "intelligences" in plural – among which artificial intelligence plays a, not absolute, role – and a better clue about the potential stretching of the intelligences we build by design.

Intelligible because meaningful

Beyond the polysemy that marks the notion of intelligence, the semantic core of this concept reminds us about the importance of creating, sharing, and maintaining the "sense" of something. The scope of the word "intelligere" comprises the idea of acting on the basis of an intention: the idea of "meaning" something, that is, to create meaningful patterns of interaction, whose "sense" is related to the context where individuals that enter into these patterns operate. Dressing the judicial vest is a social act, because exactly in relationship to the "dressing", a certain number of expectations have legitimately arisen: the hearing starts, the behaviors of the attendees must abide to the procedure, and so forth. The intelligibility of the act "dressing the judicial dress" depends on the belief systems and the social knowledge shared by both laypeople and legal actors.

Beyond the unquestionable – and physiological – gap that opens wide between the expertise of the laypeople and that of the legal actors, both types of social actors, if taking the seat in a cinema and watching the movie "12 Angry Men", will understand the sense of the acts that are "performed" within judicial rituals. The degree of this act of understanding is so high, beyond the differential distribution of specialized expertise, that they both leave the cinema with a personal assessment of what happened in the film. This simple interaction is very telling about the nature of intelligence that is embedded in the justice system. If we take seriously the insight gained from this situation we must acknowledge that 1) grasping the sense of a judicial act is a social act; 2) the social nature of this act is related to the common sense we have of the specific function performed by the justice system in a society; and 3) common sense is irrigated by the intelligence embedded into the institutions, simplified and prototyped.

Alongside the entire judicial procedure the combination of gestures and rituals, together with words and "performative" (Austin 1975) formulas, creates a distinctive tissue of sense: most of the time – as in the case of an acting scene referring to a trial in the movie – gestures, rituals, and space organization bear the heavy load of transferring within the tokens of the procedure – each trial – the meaning of each type of step that the procedure foresees for the type of trial that is celebrated. In many respects, this is the locum of silence. Etymologically, the allure of the notion of silence reflects the root of living together under conditions of peaceful settlement of disputes and conflicts: derived from the Latin word "silere", the most ancient etymology leads back to the Sanskrit, "si-legare", "to link". Therefore, it will not come as a surprise the fact that within the silence, as a sociological and socio-legal phenomenon, there is a deep root of justice.

In the analysis of the demand of justice and the relationship that links society to the law and the institutions of the justice system, silence is beyond any doubt the great absence. Neglected either because it is hard to measure the silence, or because the silence is by definition non-determined, silent dimensions of complex social and institutional phenomena, such as the law and the justice, are most of time left apart. Yet, the tacit dimension of the justice system becomes of utmost importance when one comes to assess the sources of people's trust towards the justice system. In a way, the persistency of these tacit dimensions plays the same role that Gustav Mahler recognized in the tradition, temple of the fire, rather than of the ashes. This fire, to stick to the metaphor, is the mechanism that creates a sense intelligible for many about the situation of each person. Trust has something to do with the capacity to understand, most of the time without a word on what's going on. This tacit dimension is embedded also in the trust people have for the legal services and those actors that are providing them. Between the client and the lawyer, a tacit agreement of trust goes from the first towards the second on the basis of a certain number of conditions, most of which are symbolic and institutional in their own nature.

The same type of semantic dimension of the notion of intelligence – meaning something which is intelligible and makes sense to someone or to many – is tightly related to the judicial writing or the legal writing. Drafting a legal text presenting and claiming the proofs in a civil proceeding is a socio-legal act: it is performed according to a set of norms that ensures that 1) what is written is eligible to be considered as a meaningful piece in the wide context of one proceeding; 2) the context that is meant by the legal representative is described in such a manner to be intelligible also for the opponent's legal representative and for the opponent her/himself; and 3) the ensemble of the texts written within the frame of a proceeding will make sense for other judicial and legal actors, notably at the level of the appeal, in case one of the two parts decide to appeal, and at the level of the supreme court. In case this is admitted by the civil procedural code and one of the two parts opts to reach up to the supreme court with the lawsuit. Here the role played by the verbal language is crucial, even though it is not wholly comprehensive. The organization of the text itself channels not only the institutionalized meaning of writing a text that is "judicially valid", but also the context-related sense of a specific structure of the arguments the legal and judicial actors decide to opt for.

The complexity of these two aspects, how a text is structured and how it is drafted, are vital loci to be observed and investigated if one wants to understand the intelligence within the justice system: writing, arguing, and opting for one word or for a different one are all choices and expressions of the human agency featured by the justice system. These choices gain a sense and a meaning to the professional group, the general public, and society. These are parts of the overall "audience" of the judicial ritual. Among the audiences the peers come first. Over the last decade, however, open criticism has been addressed towards the too complex and opaque structure of rulings as well as towards the its impenetrability.

There is something very true in the words of Sonia Sotomayor when she deems vital, "never to forget the real world consequences of the decisions". Among these consequences is the of channelling a meaning that speaks to the broader dimension of people (Sotomayor 2009).

In the last 20 years the request to make the "justice" system more readable to non-experts has become increasingly salient, not only in Italy. The issue is indeed very important. There are at least three reasons: transparency facilitates control; the possibility of understanding the "justice" system and its logics facilitates a better adaptation of the demand and supply of justice; communication with the citizen is a quality parameter of public administration which justice cannot escape.

In many international and national offices, it has increasingly been stressed that the citizen is the key interlocutor in architecture, legitimizing the exercise of jurisdiction; architecture in which technical and legal competence certainly plays a fundamental, necessary, but not sufficient role. Conversely, in fact, it is precisely that competence which can constitute, if not governed through organizational methods of operation, a barrier for those from outside who want to understand the reasons that underlie a judicial decision. As shown in many authoritative researches in social psychology and sociology of law, what the citizen asks for in the law and in the justice system is first of all fairness in the method of decision, fairness that also counterbalances the effect of a decision on the unsuccessful party. Being placed in a position to understand what the judge decided and why appears to be a key element in the complex articulation of the dimensions of the quality that justice should enjoy. The citizen placed before the "justice" system is not measured only by the technicality of legal language.

There are other barriers to understanding and the possibility of verifying which organizational logics govern the production of a public service, that of doing justice. For example, only a limited number of offices have adopted, as a consolidated practice, publishing the trend of office expenditure. A further example refers to the different standards and practices that are followed to draft legal and judicial documents. In the same vein, it has become evident the importance of collecting and analysing data according to standardized procedures that hold for all courts in a country. The introduction of the recent reporting technique, called the social responsibility report, opens an important but not conclusive passage in the opaque box of justice office expenses.

These are just few examples pointing out the overall need to ensure that the information about the justice system is recorded in the same format and is built alongside a standardized and transparent path, to enable both the laypeople and the institutional actors that serve within the system to develop an evidence-based understanding of the functioning of the justice institutions.

That the international discourse regarding the quality of justice unfolds between two poles – at least – that is, the emphasis on the importance of equal treatment and the emphasis on the performance of public institutions – is a consolidated fact in the analysis of literature. Scholars are unanimous in affirming that it is precisely the transition from an exquisitely formal vision to a functional – de facto – vision of the justice system that has allowed a better and deeper appreciation of the importance of access and efficiency, without neglecting the connections that link the characteristics of the mechanisms that regulate access to justice to the characteristics of the performance of the entire system (OCDE 2019).[1]

The reasoning underlying recognizing the importance of equal access and "readability" from the outside unfolds in the following ways. In general, public information and communication policies have an effect of improving the conditions of equality of access. The drafting quality of the acts is also linked to a tension, certainly shared in Europe, but in general at an international level, towards a more efficient justice. These are the points brought to the attention in the discussion tables and in the development of international standards: the differentiation of the drafting arguments structures leads to an increase in time in flow management; the lack of attention to editorial rationalization induces a "bottleneck" risk in the appeal; technology is under tension with the lack of rationalization of drafting techniques (semantic analysis by cluster of jurisprudence databases).

The relevance of the theme, transversally to the different systems and to the different trajectories traced by the reforms of the justice systems, is evidenced by the plurality of initiatives of which the most important ones are exemplified. In Germany, the Bundestag launches a stream to detect citizens' perception and access to the language of legislative and jurisprudential texts. In Spain, the Escuela Judicial witnessed the increased sensibility of institutions to the issue of "access to the language". In France, the governmental administrative simplification committee since 2002 has acted with a view to detecting access barriers (access intended as intelligibility) and in 2017 the Supreme Court of Cassation adopted a regulation setting new standards of parsimony in the legal drafting. In Canada, a wide number of experiences grew in a fertile terrain, where a "one stop front office" performs the function of the triage and the orientation to the benefit of the broad public. This is, as an example, featured by the strategy promoted in Quebec by the Centre de Justice de Proximité du Grand Montréal.[2] Operating in a multi-cultural and multilinguistic region (Quebec), the CJPGM offers on a permanent basis a "palette" of services ranging from mere information, to more specific

---

1 One important point made within this approach consists in claiming for a more differentiated access – different legal needs may be met by different mechanisms – which turns into a higher capacity for the justice system, as a whole, to deal with the different demands of justice and legal services and therefore to perform better overall. Functional differentiation must be combined with the guarantees of equal treatment for similar cases. This shifts the focus of the justice policies from a purely procedural approach – and the related formal notion of equality – towards a more functional approach – and the related notion of actual equal and fair treatment of each case.

2 "Le CJPGM est un organisme à but non lucratif ayant pour mission de promouvoir l'accès à la justice en favorisant la participation des citoyens, par des services

orientation in cases of disputes, to a broader service of public awareness. In the same vein, the recently launched ADAJ, a multi-annual project centred on the University of Montreal and combining policy-oriented research to training and professional follow-up for lawyers and judicial actors, is specifically focused on the notion of access and the related goal of dismantling the barriers to the access, among which stands out the lack of information and orientation among the general public.

It is worth noting that the relationship between the quality of judicial documents and the quality of justice is thus framed in a perspective of interdependencies. The assumptions that inspire this approach are simple, but, as a whole, are full of consequences both on an organizational and professional level. First of all, the rationalization of the structure of a judicial act produces a "quality" that does not specifically denote that act. If in fact rationalization is, therefore, a shared governance policy of the forms with which the justice system "communicates" internally and externally, then the quality that derives from this policy is an overall quality. It is therefore a matter of thinking about the single act within a system, in which it contributes, for the part of its competence, to the supply chain procedurally and both through the instances of the rite and the levels of jurisdiction. Second, it is assumed that the legibility of an action is a construction of meaning not only within the system – in this case that of justice – within which this action takes place, but also and perhaps even more towards the systems on which actions of the "generator" system has an impact. It is precisely because the actions of the justice system produce a regulatory sense of social and economic behavior that they must be able to be understood even by those who do not have specialist technical-juridical skills.

Intelligent because organized

As mentioned in the first chapter, managerial tools and performance measuring exercises championed promoting a new vision of the quality of justice from the late 20th to the early 21st century. The concept of accountability reached its apogee.[3] The intuition underpinning all accounting practices, namely the cognitive and practical advantages gained from making human affairs measurable, goes as far back as Weber's work on capitalist society, whose calculative attitude would have not been even possible if accounting in monetary terms had not been conceived and accordingly put into daily practices (Ahrne, Brunsson, and Garsten 2000). What is constitutive of accounting is an instrumental rationality,

d'information juridique, de soutien et d'orientation, offerts en complémentarité avec les ressources existantes" (CJPGM 2019).

3 For an overview and a proposal refer to Piana, 2010, chapters 2 and 3

whose drive comes from the effort of matching current reality with individual – or collective – ends by means of a number of changes. Changes might consist in actions touching upon reality and thereby transforming it. Reforms, for instance, can be understood as means enacted by public institutions aiming at improving the fitness rate between expected reality and reality as it is. However, accounting practices gained broader space over the decades than they had been awarded by Weber's work. First it came in the private sector, by means of managerial accounting. Budget people, as Argyris calls them, have drawn from this a spectacular power made out of their specialized know-how in measuring, segmenting organizations and productive cycles, calculating, and forecasting performance increase/decrease rates). This general approach turns out to be fairly challenging and challenged when accounting practices are applied to political and administrative institutions. If anything, we have all learnt from organizational studies, across political science, sociology, anthropology, and psychology, that institutions are complex and multiple-faced entities, where formal rules, roles, procedures to assign tasks, sanctions, and rewards are interlaced, if not imbricated, with informal ones (March and Olsen 1989). These latter are then embedded in the way institutions classify things, in the ways they set down their own way to frame reality and to speak about the target of their institutional actions (Douglas 1986). History provides us with countless examples where we see the apparently same policy target changing as a chameleon under new frames, ideas, policy paradigms. Policies themselves are reshaped accordingly: security and public order does not mean always the same thing in different times and locations. Welfare and social security policies are also refocused continuously as far as social reality changes and ideas about social reality change as well. Accounting, being based on quantitative measurement and quantitative assessment, desperately needs an objective conception of reality (Miller and O'Leavy 1987; Miller, 2001). Accountable objects should be easily visible to human eyes, easily detectable, and, most importantly, easily traceable. Traceability is key in this perspective. When reformers and policy makers come to act on an object – such as a system of court management – the fact of representing this object in quantitative terms enables the policy makers to consider the "object" (which is the target of their action) as the "same" during the entire process of the policy. This means, for instance, that in the quantitative representation of this object at time t1 and time t2, the same features are considered and diachronic comparison is made possible. Changes are, accordingly, represented as the sequence of a shift featured by each of the numbers (indicators), rather than being represented as a complex pattern of interaction where the object is constantly transformed not only in the quantities, but also in the qualities.

If this approach is abandoned, the correspondence between a change in the formal rules and a change in the substantial performance of the institution can't be questioned or be considered as uncertain or vague. If this would be the case, the instrumental rationality would try to reduce as much as possible the gap between the expected linear causality and the knowledge policy makers have of it.

Without indulging in easy criticisms addressed to an unquestionably important policy paradigm, which has been the leading force in shaking deeply rooted and sclerotized wisdoms and practices in public administration, some points raised by scholars, practitioners, and policy makers are nonetheless worth considering. Surely flagging the idea of replacing public bureaucracies, accused of unacceptable inefficiency and ineffectiveness, with a transparent, fully rational, and perfectly accountable costs-benefit optimizing system (Millett 1954; Davis, Kingsbury and Merry 2010) has been forced to admit its failures (Eymeri-Douzans 2005).

Experiences of institutional design, both in advanced and in developing democracies, showed that ex ante designed institutions may be shortcoming in addressing real problems once they are in place and, ex post, strictly quantitative evaluation is very unlikely in being able to explain either the success or the lack of success (Bouckaert 1993).[4] The opacity of the innovation processes then, praised by new public management-inspired practitioners and experts, creates a source of interference into a perfectly designed process of accountability. This latter is supposed to enhance the public sector's performance by means of a number of policy instruments, all based on a simple yet powerful idea: output rationality can be ensured through transparency, clear division of labour, selective incentives, and an objective approach to decision-making (Kamensky 1993; Heinrich 2002).

As long as the objectivity was strictly related to the idea of a standardized system of goal-oriented decision-making, rationality was ascribed to the role of institutional delivering. Efficient knowledge management and transparent institutions were deemed to turn into a rational system of public services deliverance (Peters 1997).

Despite these differences, once singled out, standard practices of quality management need to be put into motion in daily life. This directly touches upon a critical point raised by scholars. Accounting is, among other things, a collective activity of sense-making (Czarniawska 2008). Moreover, accounting through common standards is subjected to "local variations in activities constituting best practices" (Baxter and Chua 2009,

---

4 The position express in Peters, B.G. (2005), 'Back to the Centre?: Rebuilding the State,' in A. Gamble and T. Wright (eds), 'Restating the State,' Special Issue, The Political Quarterly 130–41 is extremely timely.

p. 68). Therefore, standards of quality management, out of which audit and accounting look prominent practices ensuring institutional performance, will become practices of good management only in relation to and dependently on the context where they will be applied and implemented. This requests a bridge that is to be built in context, not *in vacuum*.

In many countries, whereas institutional reforms, impinging upon the judicial governance, such as judicial appointment, promotion, disciplinary control and removal of judges and prosecutors, are handled exclusively by the central government and parliament, organizational innovations can be introduced at the level of the judicial office under the responsibility of the chief justice or the chief prosecutor. For example, the introduction of a front desk for the public, the human resource management system, the e-filing facilities, and so on, belong to the agenda of the local institution. Therefore, the connection between the local institution – a court of first instance, as an example, or a public prosecutor office – and the judicial networks working on the list of best practices that should be adopted to improve the court management goes through an individual tie, linking the chief justice or prosecutor and the representative in the judicial network. In some cases they are the same person, because once appointed as representative in the judicial network, the judge or the prosecutor maintains their office.

Beyond learning: the gap artificial intelligence will not fill

The promise made by the digital transformation bets on the advantages featured by a justice system whose "intelligence" incorporates artificial intelligence. This is the meaning associated with the idea of the augmented intelligence of a justice system that integrates the new devices provided by both applied mathematics and information sciences. For as simple as this promise may sound, it fits with the wide and urgent need for a more responsive justice for all and, for that reason, looks like a promising medication to the growing gap that opens wide the connection between laypeople and justice systems. The point made in this chapter suggests watching in a slightly different direction if we want to grasp effectively the effects generated by the interplay between the digital infrastructures and the justice systems. A more advantageous perspective is provided by the following guiding question: to what extent and how do the new kinds of intelligence that are embedded in the digital infrastructures – either technologies or automated rationalities, such as the algorithms – impact on the intelligence that is embedded into the justice systems? This intelligence is of a different kind, as depicted above. It relates directly with the professionalism of the legal providers, the legal consultants, the judicial actors, and the administrative staff. To what extent are these kinds of intelligence timely and salient in the digital age? Beside this question, another must be raised. This is related to the embedded intelligence that is living as organizational tacit know-how, as scripts that govern the inter-services dialogue and collaborations – such as within the courts – but also, even more significantly, for the laypeople – as scripts that govern the interface between law and the legal professions. They play the role of translators and mediators not only within the process of the dispute settlement. They also play the role of translators and mediators between the information channelled through the legal texts, the legal facts, the judicial behaviors – such as the rulings – and laypeople's needs. To some extent, this function gains exponential importance in the digital age. Laypeople are exposed to a wide number of sources of information, whose contents may be accessible. This entails, in a way, new opportunities for laypeople to find the right path to the right place to ask about legal services and justice responses, but, by the same token, laypeople will need increasing awareness to distinguish sound and not sound information, to acknowledge professionally accountable legal experts.

On the side of legal and judicial professionalism, digital transformation and the consequential range of possibilities that processes of machine learning may be applied to case law dataset, to legal texts, and judicial acts, represents an unprecedented challenge. This challenge may be won, however, by adopting a double-faced strategy. On the one hand, the *maîtrise* of methodologies capable of summarizing in deliberative and decisional reasoning tests and elements drawn from expert systems of nature different, from the expert ones, to those of an automated mathematical character, must be handled by legal and judicial actors. On the other hand, the design and the development of new kinds of intelligence, which comprise extra-legal rationalities, such as technological rationale, computational rationale, as well as information sciences, must be carried out in a collaborative context that integrates the contribution of the intelligence that is embedded in the justice systems. This point is going to be raised again and developed in Chapter 6.

References

Ahrne, G., Brunsson, N. and Garsten, C. "Standardization through organization", in *A World of Standard*, edited by N. Brunsson and B. Jacobsson, Oxford: Oxford University Press, pp. 50–68, 2000.

Austin, J. How to Do Things With Words, Harvard, Harvard University Press 1975

Baxter, J. and Chua, F. W. "Studying accountability in action: The challenge of engaging with management accounting practice", in *Accounting, Organizations and Institutions*, edited by C. Chapman, D. Cooper, and P. Miller, Oxford: Oxford University Press, pp. 65–84, 2009.

Bouckaert, G. "Measurement and meaningful management", *Public Productivity and Management Review*, 1993, 17(1): 31–43.

Calvino, I. *Palomar, Torino: Einaudi, 1983*, trans. to English: Mr Palomar, London: The Harvest Book, 1986.

Centre de Justice Proximité, Pour une justice plus accessible, Rapport Annuel, 2019-2020, Montreal, www.justicedeproximite.qc.ca/wp-content/uploads/2020/06/Rapportannuel_CJPGM_2020-VFweb3_compress.pdf

Czarniawska, B. *A Theory Of Organizing*, Cheltenham, UK: Edward Elgar Publishing, 2008.

Dallara, C. and Piana, D. *Networking the Rule of Law*, London: Ashgate, 2015.

Davis, K., Kingsbury, B., and Merry, S. "Indicators as technology of global governance", Institute for International Law and Justice, Working Papers, 2, 2010.

Douglas, M. *How Institutions Think*, Syracuse, NY: Syracuse University Press, 1986.

Eymeri-Douzans, J. M. "La gouverne au miroir du néo-management public", *Politique et Management Public*, 2005, 23(3): 1–18.

Ginsburg, T. *Judicial Review in New Democracies*, Cambridge: CUP, 2009.

Heinrich, C. "Outcomes-based performance management in the public sector: Implications for government accountability and effectiveness", *Public Administrative Review*, 2002, 62(6): 712–725.

Jean, J-PP. *L'administration de la justice en Europe et l'évaluation de sa qualité.* Paris: Dalloz, 2005.

Kamensky, J. M. "Program performance measures: Designing a system to manage for results", *Public Productivity & Management Review*, 1993, 16(4), Fiscal Pressures and Productive Solutions: Proceedings of the Fifth National Public Sector Productivity Conference (Summer, 1993), pp. 395–402.

March, J. G. and Olsen, J. P. *Rediscovering Institutions: The Organizational Basis of Politics*, New York: Free Press/Macmillan, 1989.

Miller, P. "Governing by Numbers: Why Calculative Practices Matter", *Social Research*, 2001, 68(2): 379–396.

Miller, P. and O'Leavy, T. "Accounting and the construction of the governable person", *Accounting, Organizations and Society*, 1987, 12, 235–265.

Millett, J. *Management in the Public Service.* New York: McGraw Hill, 1954.

OCDE Equal Access to Justice for Inclusive Growth: Putting People at the Centre, Éditions OCDE, Paris, available at: https://doi.org/10.1787/597f5b7f-en, 2019.

Opinion n°10 on Council for the Judiciary in the service of society, 2007.

Pauliat, H. "Le modèle française d'administration de la justice", *Revue française d'aministration publique*, 2007, 125: 111–120.

Peters, G. "Policy transfers between governments: The case of administrative reforms", *West European Politics*, 1997, 20(2): 22–36.

Piana, D. "The power knocks on the courts' back-door: Two waves of post-communist judicial reforms", *Comparative Political Studies*, 2009, 42(6): 816–840.

Piana, D. *Judicial Accountabilities in New Europe*, London: Ashgate, 2010.

Sotomayor S., A Conversation with U.S. Supreme Court Justice Sotomayor, https://2019.alaannual.org/speaker/sonia-sotomayor

Vigour, C. *Les reformes de la justice en Europe*, De Boeck, Louvain la Neuve and Paris 2018.

5 Leverages of change in the justice system

Theories that make the difference

"We delight in the beauty of the butterfly but rarely admit the changes it has gone through to achieve that beauty": these evocative words by Maya Angelou contain an unquestionable truth. The epiphenomenon takes a shape that resists all sorts of reductionism. This statement is different from the very well-known statement that claims "2 is more than 1+1". This last statement takes an anti-reductionist stance regarding the static reality: by aggregating the information one has and summing it up, one does not reach a truthful picture of reality. The point this chapter aims to make is rather different: it refers to the interdependence features of a complex interlace of processes of change impacting on several dimensions of a system. To go back to Angeleou's metaphor, we grasp the whole picture of the ensemble – the butterfly – and we, by the same token, face the complexity of the processes of change preceding the appearance of the ensemble.

The key word in this context is interdependence. Interdependence is a complicated thing to study. This statement holds even for social and political scientists who devote their energies to unpack it with obstinacy. Interdependence resists monistic and reductionist lenses. It works as a "generator of cognitive entropy": in a way it looks like when one believes they have found the edge of the puzzle, and then the puzzle changes shape. So, one must start the analysis again.

In a non-technical way, interdependence is what happens when individual actions generate consequences which, in an uncontrollable way, give rise to new phenomena. This new phenomenon, afterwards, is going to have an impact on the situations where individual actions take place.

From the practical point of view, the recognition of the interdependence leads us to take the responsibility for the consequences generated for each individual action. Above all, the recognition of interdependence solicits a new method to govern systems that are undergoing comprehensive processes of change.

If one steps back and observes from far the overall picture of the ample array of policies and strategies that have been adopted by the international organizations and transnational networks to promote, first, the rule of law, and, later, the quality of justice, one will easily discover that behind the words, the official narrative, and the deployment of tools that, as a consequence, have followed, endorses a theory of change. The theory of change belongs to the broader spectrum of the "regime of connaissances" (Commaille 2020): it is made of several components, epistemological and methodological in their nature. These components consist into a theory of agency, a theory about "how actors change their behavior and their beliefs", a theory about what is "learning", and a theory about the cutting edge between change and continuity.

A fundamental matrix: equality as the core issue

For decades, the "rule of law-equality" matrix has been addressed by international practitioners and policy makers engaged into the rule of law promotion (Merryman 1979; Trubek 2004; Cotterrell 2006). The link between the two sides of the coins, rule of law and equality, has been observed from different normative and methodological perspectives. Even recently, an interesting work (Botero, Pinzon Rondon, and Pratt 2016) has pointed to the correlation between the rule of law and individual wellbeing, the latter being assessed against standards of life expectancy, child mortality rate, and health. This quantitative analysis follows along the same line traced already by previous studies, which aimed to show that a fair and transparent legal environment is strongly correlated to the economic development and, by those means, to better living standards (Haggard, MacIntyre, and Tiede 2008; Botero Pinzon Rondon, and Pratt 2016). The development of a transnational and supranational institutional setting, comprising the whole range of different domestic justice and judicial systems that are featured by the national members, triggered a deep and wide process of policy change touching primarily on the legal and the institutional conditions to mutual recognition among authorities situated in different contexts.

Far from being uncontested, these works reveal a widespread attention for the relationship that exists between rule of law and equality. Yet, very little empirical investigation has been unfolded on the access to justice-equality interconnection. Surely, on the normative and prescriptive level, the relationship between the two (the formal and institutional guarantees of equality before the law and the equal access to the justice system) is accepted worldwide. In practical terms, laypeople should be equal before the law and, consequently, before access to the court systems, whereby the laws are enforced.

Still, between the mainstream policy discourse and empirical evidence researchers highlight concerning the relationship that ties laypeople and the justice system, a further aspect deserves some attention. Laypeople do not only demand "blind" access to justice: this may be the case if their social representation of the justice system is reconstructed, having a societal level of observation. Once the observation digs into a more context-sensitive approach, the demands of equal access appear more articulated, differentiated, and fragmented to some extent. Equal access is expected to be equal on the basis of the Aristotelian principle of equal treatment for equal items, which brings us directly to the key argument developed in Chapter 3, that is, the demand of justice is, as a matter of fact, made by the many demands of many different legal services.

Empirical observations of trials and qualitative analysis of the experiences encountered within the courthouses as well as at the entrance – to quote a Kafka metaphor, of the "castle of the law" – seem to reveal, however, that this relationship is far from being genuine. Better still, in sociopolitical contexts where the formal guarantees of an impartial and impersonal application of the law are well established, it is not assured that laypeople have *in fact* equal opportunities to receive an equal answer from the justice system. In this case "equal" means: equally predictable, equally certain in terms of timeframe and readability, equally promptly and certainly executed (Sandefur 2019; Agrast et al. n.d; Piana 2016). For laypeople, this dimension of equality is as important as the formal dimension. It is so even more for those laypeople that are situated in less favourable conditions (Verdonschot 2008).

To ensure equal treatment before the law and equal protection of individual rights, all institutions endowed with authoritative competences should be subjected to the law. Hence, far beyond any cultural differences and historical trajectories, the rule of law as an institutional ideal is about "limit the exercise of power". One of the axes along which the *European norms* limit the exercise of power is the one that links the European level of rights enforcement with the national level of policy making. In most cases, these norms are legal in nature.

These remarks explain the linkage between rule of law promotion and quality of justice enhancement, on the one hand, and the notion of equality assumed in the official narratives that frame the promotion policies and the enhancement strategies. The critical role played by the notion of equality – and the scope this notion has from the semantic point of view – gets a distinctive significance in the context of the European Union. For almost an entire decade European institutions have been confronted with the titanic enterprise of defining a core of concepts, principles, and goals which have a high probability of being accepted by all the member states, despite the cultural and institutional differences. When the concept of quality of justice made its appearance the first goal it was expected to reach was setting the ground for an inter-governmental debate on the functioning of the judicial systems. Starting from the early 2000s, the European institutions embarked upon a comprehensive process of rule-making, the nature of which is not statutory but, rather, practical. The norms that are shaped through this process belong to the ideal type of "soft law". Despite the variegated nature of the soft law – encompassing several different sub-types of normative tools – one may safely argue that soft laws are not legally binding and therefore their capacity to impinge upon institutional decision-making is intimately related to the will of actors that endorse these norms as normative principles or behavioral models. Soft laws are guidelines showing the way a court should be managed, benchmarks fixing the reasonable timeframe of a trial at the first instance and at the appeal, models of IT-based case management, models of judicial training, models judicial governance, guidelines and recommendations upon the interaction between the courts and the media, the courts and the society, the judge and the prosecutor, and so on.

This growing set of inputs is non-legally binding, since the European institutions, and not the EU or the Council of Europe, have jurisdiction upon the organization of the state of their members. The "soft" nature of these inputs has its roots here. It is with these considerations in mind that one should observe the work of the European Commission for the Efficiency of Justice (CEPEJ). The *Resolution* of the Committee of Ministers of the Council of Europe that set up the CEPEJ in 2002 reads: "recognizing that the on which European democracies rest cannot be ensured without fair, efficient and accessible judicial systems". The *Resolution* refers to the macro themes that have occupied the core of the CEPEJ's agenda ever since: 1) access to justice and proper and efficient functioning of courts; 2) the status and role of the legal professionals; 3) administration of justice and management of courts; 4) use of information and communication technologies. These four items are permanently on the menu of the CEPEJ's meetings and works. The *Resolution* also refers to a "normative anchor" (Morlino 2011) which consists of the European Convention of Human Rights arts 5 and 6 and creates a semantic bridge between the abstract and universal principle of "fair trial" and the concrete and practical conditions where courts operate.

The premise which stands at the basis of the CEPEJ's creation claims that the right to a fair trial, stated in the ECHRs, will be undermined or not fully enforced if the judicial offices are not capable of ensuring equal access to the administration of justice to all laypeople, if they do not ensure a reasonable time frame, if they do not administrate efficiently and effectively the human resources they dispose of, and finally if they do not rely on a solid and reliable implementation of IT tools. These latter are instrumentally valuable, since they might be very effective in reducing the backlogs, in speeding up the length of the proceedings, in making more easily accessible for users and laypeople the services of the courts, and so on. In short, the CEPEJ has been vested with the responsibility of intervening within the judicial systems of the states, without being vested with the authority of sanctioning the states that do not follow its recommendations through. The CEPEJ is not conceived as a supervisory body either. Therefore, the relationship that is set up between the CEPEJ and the states is not the one that can be worded in terms of hierarchy. The mechanism of influence, consequently, does not work with a top-down scheme of governance.

Socio-legal research carried out through fieldwork in the jurisdictions, comparative analysis of policy-making processes unfolded within the justice systems, and experts' reports provide an overall picture of the achievements reached by means of these actions which question seriously the theory of change that is endorsed therein. While the adoption of targeted measures enhancing the efficiency and the effectiveness of court administration proved to give relief to those domestic systems that have been overloaded by an increasing litigation and a consequent backlog (Piana 2016), the correlation between the improvement of the quality of justice and the above mentioned policies is less than genuine.

Certainly, the rule of promotion policies left us an important legacy: impartial courts are crucial conditions to enhance the human development and the political stability of all societies. However, justice systems and demands for justice go far beyond the scope targeted by the adjudication and judicial decisions. Informal justice systems coexist beside – and somehow interact with – the court-based systems. Extra-judicial mechanisms of dispute resolution started to play an important role in responding to the demand for right enforcement and, for other reasons and for a specific group of actors, arbitration has gained a primary position among the possible methods companies can opt for to settle a dispute. A somehow spontaneous convergence can be detected between, on the one hand, the empirical research conducted in the field of policy analysis, administrative and organizational science, and the development of a richer and more comprehensive approach at the international scale, on the other. The point of convergence can be shortly worded as follows: legal leverages and organizational leverages, both targeting the courts' functioning, are necessary conditions for the enforcement of the rule of law.

Yet the justice delivered to laypeople stems not only from the court system but also from an articulated, multi-dimensional, and inter-dependent system, ranging from the legal and regulative framework to the legal services to the courts, to the execution of the judicial decisions. In short, theories of change that lie at the basis of the quality of justice promotion paradigm are questioned with regard to their hypotheses about the mechanisms of change and the leverages of change. The question that remains largely unanswered is: What works? And why is it so?

Governing change with standards

As we have shown, justice systems for several decades have been ranked at the top of the international agenda on good governance, inclusive growth, poverty reduction, and equal treatment promotion. Despite the specific aspects of the countries, the political contingencies, the different legal cultures, and the models of judicial governance, domestic policies have all been marked by a significant and relentless attempt to improve the justice systems by adopting new laws and injecting new input into the organizational units of the courts, the public prosecutor offices, the bars, and, in general, in all institutions that are co-participants in the *mise en oeuvre* of the rule of law principle within the justice sector.

This has happened so far by means of two types mechanisms:

- Legal provisions and promotion of legal tools
- Standard setting and promotion of soft law-inspired reforms.

The two mechanisms go hand in hand with two qualitatively different methods of rule-adoption and rule-implementation. Legal provisions are adopted by codified legal procedures. These provisions will be more effectively implemented if at the basis of the implementation lies a substantial engagement of the different agencies, institutional actors, services, and professional groups whose scope of action and whose behaviour are affected by these provisions. The key word in this context is engagement. This entails not simply a participation either to the design of the provision – legal drafting – or to the mise en oeuvre of the policies that stems from the adoption of this provision. It is rather a matter of "engagement as a method based on a cycle of policy design, implementation, and evaluation", which creates a virtuous cycle of mutual and recursive learning and improvement. Just to provide an example: a reform of the civil procedural code is first drafted by a legislative service within the ministry of justice, debated behind closed doors by the council of ministers, shared and discussed with the stakeholders in some cases, and then put through the parliamentary process of amendments and adoption (Knill 2001).

The standard-based approach has been promoted also to medicate these problems and to avoid these costs. Standards are shaped without the need for going through the parliamentary processes and political transactions entailed by these. Standards are, moreover, derived from practices that have been experienced and have proven on the field their effectiveness and their sustainability. At the same time, standards are general rules, they are worded in abstract terms. If one states that "the courthouses should adopt reliable mechanisms to communicate in a user friendly manner with the laypeople", this statement reads in an abstract and general enough manner to then be incorporated into several different possible contexts and still contains important normative meanings (reliable is a normatively connoted term).

The strategy, which consists of governing courts by standards, is fairly popular in most international organizations, such as the World Bank and the OECD (Grindle 2011). In Europe, the enterprise of constructing uniformities across legal and judicial boundaries still overlapping national political and geographical boundaries looks to be a fairly titanic venture, entailing a paramount volume of work. The concept of "quality of justice" seems to have rephrased the concept of the rule of law by adding to the impartial and lawful adjudication of other principles, such as the actual possibility of being able to access the court system, the transparency of court management, and the efficiency of the resource management scheme adopted by courts. A high number of non-legally binding norms has made its appearance in the European Union as one of the most path-breaking outcomes of a transnational standard-setting process targeting the administration and organization of domestic courts and public prosecutor offices. Several types of standards have been put forth: reasonable timeframe, equal access to justice, efficient financial management, effective public communication, and so on (Fabri et al. 2005).

In order to ensure both the measurement and (consequently) the quantitative assessment of the judicial systems concepts such as "timeframe", "delays", and "fair trial" have been unpacked and translated into indicators. The operationalization of the quality of justice came as a new avenue to compare systems that proved to be fairly reluctant to mere integration or yet quite different and diver-gent in terms of their own strategies to go about court overloading and challenging cases (involving children, refugees, or ethical and religious issues). In general, if, by any chance, a European citizen had the oppor-tunity to observe the European judicial systems from an external point of view, say a planet of the solar system, s/he would be in the position to spot huge differences in the way trials take place and surely in the way the law is used, applied, and enforced. Differences do not refer here to legal norms. Rather it refers to the organization, the staff, the services offered to users, and the number of mechanisms of public and social accountability under which judicial staff are held. In this context the road which consists in unfolding standard-settings processes needs to be accompanied by a long process of operationalization, which creates a set of nominal labels (indicators) to allocate different things with similar names:

> An indicator is a named, rank-ordered representation of past or projected performance by different units that uses numerical data to simplify a more complex social phenomenon, drawing on scien-tific expertise and methodology. The representation is capable of being used to compare particular units of analysis (such as coun-tries or persons), and to evaluate their performance by reference to one or more standards.
>
> (Davis, Kingsbury, and Merry 2012, p. 2)

This way of phrasing the function performed by indicators fits per-fectly with the stance taken by the monitoring institutions towards the measurement of the quality of justice and responded to their need to find a common and possibly "a-cultural" manner to speak about justice across the national borders. The idea underpinning this work can be outlined as follows: justice administration is a public sub-sector and should be held accountable from the point of view of the capacity of delivering a good service to users – laypeople – and of the capacity to allocate money along with a strict instrumental rationality.

Remedies suggested come from best practices experienced in more advanced countries – countries that rank high from the point of view of court efficiency – and from the development of common standards which serve as common transnational reference points to assess the quality of national and sub-national judicial offices. Judicial offices respectful of the rule of law should be efficient in delivering judicial decisions in due course, should be transparent in the way they manage their resources, and should introduce competent IT instruments to facilitate information processing and public communication. To put it briefly, innovation has become common sense when policy makers refer to judicial institutions and are asked to solve and medicate any weaknesses affecting the judicial sector, such as unreasonable time frame, uneasy or unfair access to the courts, lack of confidence granted by the general public to the bench, and so on (Frydman 2011).

This has entailed a growing commitment to inject within the traditional systems of judicial governance new organizational practices and policies originated in other systems or offices. The injection into a specific context of abstract models of judicial governance ends with its encapsulation or hybridization caused by cultural and organizational forces, rooted into the domestic court system (Hammergren 2005; Albers 2008).

In other words, transnational standards are forced to accommodate many different national legacies which bridge standards into practice and eventually can generate unintentional and unforeseeable effects (Ahrne, Brunson, and Garsten 2000). Hybridization and acclimatization are two different mechanisms that have been observed by scholars in several different policy contexts. One of the effects they entail consists in the creation of opportunities for micro changes in the systems where the standards are acclimatized. If in theory the standard for open access to court is set transnationally, the organization where this standard is made into a daily working practice can interpret it in several manners, if specific guidelines are not provided. It is the centre of the system which is, somehow, asked to provide bridging guidelines, transforming abstract standards into concrete organizational and communicative schemes. For sure, in the absence of of legal obligation and under conditions of semantic openness, a differential implementation, dependent on the context and the legacies, is not only possible, but even desirable. Standards and soft laws in general define the borders of legitimate policy windows, through which domestic policy makers can then intervene.

In most cases the promotion of specific solutions is based on the endorsement of a user-oriented approach that frames judicial reforms and leads them in an output-oriented direction. The actual entrepreneurship of the domestic institutions and the implementation of these types of normative inputs – that is, non-legally binding norms – depend enormously on the availability of capable actors, of legitimate and influential policy entrepreneurs, of domestic facilitating conditions in terms of political competition, and on the organizational forces at work in the judicial field. This is the reason why the analysis of a critical case, the Italian one, may cast new light upon the potential consequences – including the unintended effects – of the judicial reforms driven by the quality of justice mainstream.

Therefore, standards-based governance features a fundamental weakness: it promises equal treatment by means of a theory of change that justifies the hypothesis of setting a baseline for the justice system regardless of the specific contexts where the standards are implemented. Reality speaks differently. Once the "standard" abandons the realm of the "design" and lands on the realm of the "use in context", several factors intervene to acclimatize it: the organizational legacy, the specific legacy of the social context, the professionalism of change actors, and the vast array of tacit, but crucial cognitive and practical scripts and rules that give shape and substance to the "texture" of a justice systems.

If one seeks to apply the standard-based method to the new phenomenon that is making its appearance through the wide and deep spreading of digital technologies and computational devices applied to justice, the epistemological and methodological weaknesses that have been portrayed above jeopardize the entire strategy. The international discourse is inclined to place the burden of the regulation on the design and the applications of common standards, such as the standards that are presented in the international guidelines, blueprints, and white papers:

> "This framework is based on four key principles: enable self-determination, cultivate the commons, decentralise infrastructure and empower public institutions";[1] "based on fundamental rights and ethical principles, the Guidelines list seven key requirements that artificial intelligence systems should meet in order to be trustworthy: human agency and oversight, technical robustness and safety, privacy and data governance, transparency, diversity, non-discrimination and fairness, societal and environmental well-being, accountability";[2] in the justice sector "principle of respect for fundamental rights: ensure that the design and implementation of artificial intelligence tools and services are compatible with fundamental rights; principle of non-discrimination: specifically prevent the development or intensification of any discrimination between individuals or groups of individuals; principle of quality and security: with regard to the processing of judicial decisions and data, use certified sources and intangible data with models

---

1 https://shared-digital.eu/.
2 https://ec.europa.eu/futurium/en/ai-alliance-consultation.

elaborated in a multidisciplinary manner, in a secure technological environment; principle of transparency, impartiality and fairness: make data processing methods accessible and understandable, authorize external audits; principle 'under user control': preclude a prescriptive approach and ensure that users are informed actors and in control of the choices made".[3]

The standard-based approach is particularly promising from the point of view of the international watchdogs: it enables monitoring and regulating softly the design of the digital tools and the computational devices that are afterward adopted within the justice systems. However, the same approach falls short in ensuring that the overall outcome of the encounter between the justice systems and the digital technologies and the computational rationalities responds to the needs of laypeople, to the professional standards of several professions that are operating within the justice systems, and ultimately to the notion of "justice" that societies endorse.

To word this last point in short, one may say that the standards are introducing a scale that does not necessarily correspond to the scales of justice that is living – most of the time silently – within the interactions, the ties, and the linkages that actors within the justice systems set up and keep alive.

This remark considers two levels. The first one is the surrounding context where justice is administered. What is justice, which demands of justice are addressed to the legal services' providers, and the jurisdictions, are questions that can't remain unanswered. The second one is the pattern of interaction that exists within the justice systems, at the level of the organization of the legal services providers and at the level of the jurisdiction. Both these organizations have standing dialogues with non-legal professionalisms: consultants, technical experts, ICT experts, economic experts, and statisticians. Digital infrastructures create a window through which new professionalisms and, consequently, new standards, enter into the justice systems. The "right" method to design a digital platform is conceived on the basis of a combination of technological and legal standards. The right method to carry on a machine-learning process is defined on the basis of the mathematical standards that regulate the different technics adopted – such as the recursive technique, the classification, and so on. Which standard must come first? Is there any reason to accept that a first-ranked standard will be always first ranked? Is there any trade-off that can be preliminarily settled between compliance to the mathematical standards and compliance with the social request of transparency and intelligibility?

We deem that the answers to these questions must be found within the empirical world.

Inspiring cases

Court systems that feature a loosely coupled mechanism of centre-territories dialogue feature, at the same time, a high potential for innovation. Despite this potential not necessarily being reflected in permanent improvement, it gives origin to a vast array of experiences from which learning and imitating actions can start. This is the case of district jurisdiction that has been among the first comers in the process of digitalizing civil procedure in Europe. Two favourable conditions facilitate this innovation: the collaboration between the bar association and the judicial staff of the local jurisdiction; the well-established tradition of intra-jurisdictional dialogue among the judges, the prosecutors, and the administrative officers. These two context-related conditions played favourable intervening factors also in the recent creation of a new laboratory where artificial intelligence application to the justice system has been tested. The new experience pivots on three key pillars: the participation of the researchers and the academic teams that are operating within the local university, the participation of representatives of the bar, the judges, and the clerks to the discussions, and the works that are deployed within an executive board, the concomitant design of a comprehensive array of options to train the judges, the lawyers, and the clerks. The design of this method of governance features three characters that differentiate themselves from a purely standard-based method: first, the logic of action that is adopted responds to a combination of standards, legal, technical – the experts of data sciences and information science are members of the board as peers – organizational, and professional; second, the elaboration of the algorithm obeys a logic of transparency and of trustworthiness, which applies to both the experts and the experts/justice systems actors dialogue; third, the field of application has been selected according to an attentive and empirically based analysis of the demands of justice that feature a higher urgency and a higher sensitivity to equal treatment. The results resonate as a positive test of a participative design of governance. Where the theories of change are coming in? The theory of change that is implicitly adopted within this design relies on the assumption of two leverages of change: expected benefits that lead to adaptive behaviors and cognitive focal points that help different actors set up a process of design and use where accountability is a common experience, rather than a segmented and functionally differentiated pattern of interaction between actors and norms. This means to go beyond – and abandon – the idea of a one-to-one pattern of compliance, technical experts compliant with technical standards, legal services providers compliant with legal standards, and so forth. A further point that is worth bearing in mind relates to the leverage of change that works in the policies of transparency and participation. Instead of adopting a method of making visible the rationale of the design of the algorithm once it has been made, the method here prospects a path from the screening of legal needs to the elaboration of a machine learning process where the key steps are subjected to a participated process of answerability and accountability. This is going to create trust. Actors involved in it reply to the interviews by witnessing a high degree of trust, despite the fact that each of them sticks to their own paradigm of professionalism – judges are not asked to become experts of mathematics nor are mathematicians are asked to become legal experts. In other words, the recurrent check of the consequences and the unforeseen (nor foreseeable) consequences of the use of technological and information devices within the scope of action of lawyers, judges, and judicial institutions in general is required because the use of these devices triggers unexpected and unpredictable effects and consequences whose compliance to the principles of equality and fairness must be ensured to be "de facto" (not only in the design).

A southern jurisdiction of the European space looks like a promising field to assess the potential impact of mutual learning on the quality of the digitalization. Despite taking seriously the standard guideline that praises a paperless legal service and a digitalized docket management, the shift from a material and face-to-face pattern of daily work towards an immaterial – or partially immaterial – pattern brings new challenges, both for the bar association and the jurisdictions. Moreover, the quality of the legal services and the response to the justice demands requires a new standard of explanation. Public accountability is put under pressure. Here the twinning model appears. Twinning projects currently represent the bulk of large-scale activity in international cooperation based on bilateral exchanges between old and candidate members. In the process of enlargement, several experts moved from Western countries to Central and Eastern European countries to disseminate know-how and to bridge gaps between their own country and the host administration located in candidate countries. Even though judicial education was not included on the agenda of any project, training sessions, and exchanges of views, legal expertise (for instance, doctrine or interpretative patterns of legal norms) and ideas were somehow encouraged in each judicial cooperation project. Twinning and bilateral or multilateral cooperation projects have entailed large-scale socialization activity (Piana 2014 and 2016). Socialization and training were thus not just specific objectives of cooperative projects, but also spillover effects of other projects, most of which were based on peer review, cross-border discussion, or teaching. The role played by experts in the standard-driven policy transfer experiences can be summarized in the following way. Experts are expected to be aware of the standards and therefore handle an abstract model of what should be done under general conditions. Moreover, they are selected and appointed to the projects of judicial cooperation because of their knowledge of the system or of the organization from which the practice that should be transferred originates. They visit the beneficiary or the recipient organization and select those conditions that can facilitate the transfer or/and address those barriers that can create obstacles to the transfer. The expert operates during a short or medium timeframe in the recipient organization. A number of training sessions are foreseen to create awareness and to train the staff of the organization who, once the project reaches its end, need to be capable of managing and incorporating the new practice into their own way of doing things. The a posteriori audit showed, however, in a high number of cases that despite the quality of the design of the transfer and the quality of the practices transferred, the internalization of the norms and the translation into routinized practices easily fails. Rather than using experts as mechanisms to channel good practices inspired by standards and experienced in specific contexts, experts can be better if they work out the method of acclimatization of the standards and the monitoring tools that are necessarily put into motion to ensure the effectiveness and success of the change introduced into a justice system or a court. Method-wise, the implementation of standards features a higher sensitivity to the quality of the monitoring process and of the "in itinere" evaluation, not only at the central level (the ministry or the high judicial council or any other domestic institutions vested with the responsibility of ensuring the good governance of the justice system). The type of indicators, the scope of the observation, the timeframe and the regularity of the measurement, the tools of data analysis, and the grammar used in the successful storytelling, all these aspects are covered by the "method". They should be ensured by the experts. Beyond this, a deeper and newly shaped engagement of the actors who are the protagonists of the practices, the players that each day work in the justice systems, is necessary. This engagement is, in our understanding, conceived alongside two trajectories of reasoning: the first refers directly to the role that should be played by leaders and the second refers to the comparative method of policy transfer.

Leaders and chief justices in the justice systems play an increasingly significant role in ensuring the good governance and the quality of the services delivered to laypeople and business. In many countries, the burden of policy implementation is on them, due to the room of man-oeuvre they enjoy in the adaptation of general inputs to the organiza-tional context where they operate on a daily basis.

Once the tools and the steps are indicated and the regulation of the procedures is adopted by the ministries, the specific, punctual, micro-adaptation of the IT-based practices of work to the already-in-place practices takes place within the services and the offices, under the overarching supervision of the chief in the office. The strong engagement of leaders to make a process of change into a real success story is not unforeseen by the policy makers. We've already got it and have gained a diffuse and consensual awareness of the importance all decision-makers have to assign to this aspect. This knowledge comes from analysis of all administrative reforms, especially those that have been inspired by a result-oriented approach (Eymeri-Douzans 2013; Pëters 2012; Contini and Lanzara 2014). Less genuine is the consensus reached on the role that leaders should play in the justice sector, because this aspect touches directly upon sensitive issues such as the discretionary power that legit-imate justices and prosecutors handle and the autonomy vs the account-ability that should/are associated with the use of this power. However, the reality is such that it would be hard to deny that leaders and chiefs are front players in the implementation of all policies that are inspired by standards. A second point refers instead to the comparative method that should be adopted to ensure that the implementation costs of good practices are reduced.

The point that we want to make here is that twinning projects are very promising as avenues to translate good standards into good practices. However, they should not be designed in a vertical manner: one organ-ization experiences one practice, verifies that this is effective, then experts come, observe this practice, model it, and transfer it into a new organ-ization. It is better to ensure that a small group of staff operating in one organization observe in practice the ways of doing things in a second (twinned) organization on the basis of a grid that is designed by the experts. They learn not only the practice (how to do something), but also avoid the learning costs that have been paid by the giver – the organ-ization that had first tested the practice. Afterwards the small group injects the practice into its own organization, relying on the awareness that has been gained in the twinned organization (which has worked out as a laboratory). The same should be done bilaterally, as an exchange of practice, where the recipient organization, which benefits from the learning process unfolded in the twin, provides also in exchange a good practice, whose observation is then made by a small group coming from the first organization and observing in real-time the practice deployed in the second organization. The overarching analytical framework as well as the monitoring tool should be designed by the expert and provided once, for good, to the two organizations that need to be autonomous and self-governing in the monitoring and consolidation of the change.

This method can be qualified as integrated, combining vertical and horizontal types of learning (learning within the experiencing organization and learning between the two twinned organizations). It also combines a multiple set of expertise and competences, insiders and outsiders, actors operating in the justice systems and experts. It would be preferable to have it applied to twinned organizations rather than larger samples to reduce the transaction costs and the organizational costs in the application of the method itself. Once doubly tested and cross-checked, the practice can be also debated as a potential template for other similar organizations. The key point is represented by the selection of "similar" organizations. Mutual learning happens effectively if cognitive processes unfold accordingly. The representation of the original organization – the one from which the good practice comes and where the good practice is observed – should be conducive to sound and reliable analogies so that similar conditions facilitating the introduction of the practice can be easily pointed out. When a process of horizontal learning is in place, several features of the two institutions that engage in this process must be taken into consideration. Among these, the organizational size of the two institutions, which impinges upon monitoring costs entailed by the processes of change.

The role played by experts and consultants in the contemporary world should be highlighted once again. Knowledge is the key to making a policy idea a successful solution. Specific and reliable know-how is of utmost importance in all processes of institutional and organizational changes. This is what we have learnt from all the experiences of reforms enacted over the last decades in all advanced democracies. Less genuine is, however, the relationship between the injection of expertise and the durability of change. This holds especially in those cases of change that feature a low degree of formal constraints and rather rely on a high degree of spontaneous or at least not formal mandatory commitment. The experiences of policies adopted to improve the quality of justice under the auspices of the European institutions belong to this second type. Why are the quality of expertise and the quality of change not linearly and necessarily correlated?

This is the case for several reasons. At a first sight it is intuitively acknowledgeable that between the experts and the judicial staff that benefit from the expertise provided there exists an asymmetry of information. Surely during the period spent by the expert team in the courthouse to design the policy, to acclimatize the standards to the specific organizational context, and ultimately to teach and train the court staff, a "quantum" of knowledge is transferred not by means of declarative utterances – communications acts – but by means of imitation, emulation, and practice examples. After this period of time, however, what remains in the organization is different from what has been brought in initially, both method- and content-wise. The regular, predictable, routinized implementation of ways of doing things that mirror the standards but incorporate all micro-actions of redesign and adaptation that are requested by the context should, in principle, become part of the cognitive schemata followed by judges, prosecutors, and clerks in their daily working life. Moreover, the systemic effect triggered by the encounter of the previous organizational practices and the new ones is not fully known in advance. It is rather a matter of discovery. The discovery, in many cases, happens when the experts have left already and entails a high level of learning costs. Learning by doing is a way to bring about a process of change but it happens alongside a vertical logic. At the time the organization launches a new policy, a new tool, a new solution to a functional problem, having in mind a final goal, which usually is worded in terms of "improvement of the quality of justice", or "reduction of the trial timeframe", or "improvement of the public trust towards the judiciary". The goal is considered fixed and the process of change is launched. The gap between the expected outcomes and the actually originated results is measured along the way. This is the typical logic of a result-oriented rationality, which is not profoundly changed even if the goals and the expected results are inspired by a standard or by a normative principle that has the shape of a non-legally binding norm (such as a standard or a guideline).

How do we avoid or balance out the side effects that this avenue seems to entail? With a shift in the method of expertise provision and a change in the method of policy transfer.

"Policy transfer" is a concept that bridges the difficulties classical disciplinary perspectives have in dealing with multi-level governance and transnational regimes (Rose 1993). Policy transfer is a process by which a practice, a solution, a way of doing this or that, proven effective in a context, is then transferred into a different context. This happens alongside the recruitment of experts who are knowledgeable in both systems – the one that originates the practice and the one that benefits from its transfer. The convergence of policy instruments across national politics and the diffusion of policy solutions among domestic policy systems are increasingly common features of contemporary political processes since they seem to stem from the development of supranational sources of norms and regulations. This explains the fact that in contemporary politics, "foreign agents and institutions seem to increasingly become sources of policy ideas, policy design, and implementation". The process of European integration is an excellent empirical field within which to test the empirical adequacy of this analytical perspective because of the prominent role played by the European institutions in facilitating the exchange and circulation of best practice among member states. The EU has put extensive pressure on national governments to measure their policy failures using an international set of standards and benchmarks (Börzel and Risse 2003). The concept of "policy transfer" was not at first evident in European studies but the mere fact that policy transfer is the "methodology for making European Union policy" has opened up the possibility of exploiting this concept to explain the logic of Europeanization. Indeed, besides the mechanism of the adoption of a number of legal norms as included in the *acquis communautaire*, member states and candidate countries compare their policy styles and gauge their capacity to conform to European benchmarks. This has also pushed scholars to talk about a "new approach to policy", one which weakens the monopoly of national governments in setting their domestic agenda and which no longer uses coercive mechanisms of government (Kerver 2005).

After having explored changes in the field of policy that directly relate to the political dimension of EU decisions, scholars have also explored the changes which the process of European integration entails the structure of the state (for an overview and critique of the "research agenda"). Empirical evidence gathered so far has shown that in the policy fields in which the EU exercises "soft power", the mechanisms of influence driving institutional changes go beyond compulsory adaptation and depend also on the voluntary imitation of best practice and of successful solutions. This holds for instance in the field of judicial policy. Even though the judicialization of European politics has been studied (Trubek 2004; Stone Sweet 2002), there are few works addressing the Europeanization of domestic judicial policy, and none that address the Europeanization of judicial policies in candidate countries. In fact, the "Europeanization approach" to the candidate countries raises some analytical difficulties, such as the question as to whether the concept of "Europeanization" has the same meaning for old and for prospective member states, an issue which was first highlighted by academics (Morlino 2002). This notwithstanding, we would argue that Europeanization through policy transfer can be used to develop a deeper understanding of policy processes in candidate countries if the concept of "Europeanization" means a process of creation, selection, diffusion of normative inputs, the value of which is due to the fact that they are produced or promoted by European institutions (Radaelli 2003). This conception fits perfectly with the policy transfer framework:

"the process by which knowledge about policies, administrative arrangements, institutions and ideas in one political system ... is used in the development of policies, arrangements, institutions and ideas in another political system" (Dolowitz and Marsh 2000, 5). According to that view, the crux of the policy transfer framework becomes the comprehension of "who are the key actors involved in the policy transfer", and of "what is transferred and what restricts or facilitates the policy transfer?" (Idem).[1] Thus, we would argue that an *actor-centred view* of the process of Europeanization can account for the process of creation, selection, and diffusion of normative inputs, the appropriateness and legitimacy of which depends on the fact that they have a truly "European" feature. In that view, Europeanization is conceived as a process that has touched upon the "constellation of actors" involved in policy making across different levels of governance (Piana 2007c).

The importance of multiple networks has been already pointed out and stresses the differential impact that networks have, the differences depending on the identity of the actors who are in a position to adopt input from abroad and implement them at home. Such actors are vested with a de facto power as gate-keepers and are influenced by the pressure exercised by the supranational institutions through non-coercive instruments (Scott and Trubek 2002). As far as the Europeanization of candidate countries is concerned, scholars have identified several mechanisms of influence that go far beyond the coercion of political conditionality (Schimmelfenning and Sedelmeier 2004; Dimitrova 2005). Empirical researches have shown that social learning and lesson drawing have been channels of democratization "from abroad" for EU candidates. In particular, studies acknowledge that the European normative inputs aimed at promoting democracy and the rule of law differ considerably in terms of their compulsory force (Grabbe 2002; Closa 2016, http://eiop.or.at/eiop/; Schwellnus 2005). Where the absence of legal constraint opens the door to *social learning* (Checkel 2001) and *lesson drawing* (Rose 1993), actors involved in transfer networks are best placed to shape the process of creation, selection and diffusion of norms. Indeed, actors moving across national and supranational policy sub-systems are vested with the power of taking norms and adapting them to national institutional settings. Moreover, experts are also in the best position to fully exploit their competence to interpret inputs before they enter the domestic system (Stone 1997). In the field of judicial education, the EU is not vested with any coercive power. Norms that apply to that field are not legally binding. Thus, the diffusion of models and policy solutions tried out in other countries represents a key mechanism of Europeanization. The participation in epistemic communities involved in the process is a key variable in the process of Europeanization (as intended above) and accounts for the differences among countries equally subject to external opportunities for imitation and transfer.[13] Accordingly, the low degree of legalization (Abbott and Snidal 2000) of the "pro-rule of law" norms – the ones that become the normative guidelines for judicial education programmes – does not simply represent a pitfall in the pre-accession strategy, but can be also seen as an opportunity to test the other mechanisms that work above and beyond legal coercion. Indeed, the absence of legal constraint opens the door to an *entrepreneurship* by domestic policy makers, a phenomenon that helps the interpretation of European standards and their integration into the domestic institutional context.

The external effects of European policies take place along a continuum that runs from fully voluntary to more constrained forms of adaptation, and include a variety of modes such as unilateral emulation, adaptation by externality and policy transfer through conditionality. Accordingly, Europeanization can be conceived as a process of transformation of policy making across borders and between two levels of governance: the transnational and the national levels. It has created arenas where national policy makers can coordinate their strategies and can learn successful policies experienced in other countries. The creation of epistemic communities and policy networks working at the transnational level are exogenous incentives to policy transfer, set up by the European Union. Within this setting, policy transfer in the European space can be understood as a particular form of policy making through multi-level networks. The crucial platform that gives incentives to the process of transfer is the transfer network that is a network of actors that exchange information and ideas within a particular policy sector. Experts belonging to epistemic communities (Haas 1992), that is to say policy networks that cross national borders, are only part of a variety of transfer networks which may be set up in a multi-level system of governance. To the extent that policy makers move across the national borders and between the domestic and the European arenas, they progressively enforce the domestic ties that the policy sub-systems have with the transnational policy network.

References

Abbott, K. and Snidal, D. "Hard and soft law in international governance", *International Organization*, 2000, 54(3): 421–441.

Agrast, M., Botero, J., Martinez, J., Ponce, A., and Pratt, C. "The World Justice Project/Rule of Law Index 2012–2013", The World Justice Project, Washington, DC, n.d.

Ahrne, G., Brunsson, N., and Garsten, C. "Standardization through organization", in *A World of Standards*, edited by N. Brunsson and G. Jacobsson, Oxford: Oxford University Press, 50–68, 2000.

Albers, P. "Best practices on the prevention of the unreasonable length of proceedings: experiences of the CEPEJ", Communication presented at the UniDem Campus Seminar, organized by the Venice Commission, Trieste, 25–28 February, 2008.

Beetham, H. and Sharp, R. *Rethinking Pedagogy for a Digital Age*, London: Routledge, 2007.

Börzel, Tanja A., and Risse, T. "Conceptualising the domestic impact of Europe", in *The Politics of Europeanisation*, edited by K. Featherstone and C. Radaelli. Oxford, 55–78, 2003.

Botero, J. C. and Pinzon-Rondon, A. M., and Pratt, C. "How, When and Why Do Governance, Justice and Rule of Law Indicators Fail Public Policy Decision Making in Practice?" *Hague Journal on the Rule of Law*, 2016, 8(1): 51–74, available at SSRN: https://ssrn.com/abstract=3169342

Commaille, J. "Réformer la Justice". Quel régime de connaissance mobiliser en référence à une nouvelle théorie générale de la fonction de justice à construire? *Revue Juridique Themis*, 2020.

Cotterrell, R. *Law, Culture and Society: Legal Ideas in the Mirror of Social Theory*, Aldershot: Ashgate, 2006.

Closa, C. Reinforcing EU monitoring of the rule of Law. In: Closa C, Kochenov D (eds) Reinforc-ing Rule of Law Oversight in the European Union. Cambridge University Press, Cambridge, pp 15–35, 2016.

Davis, K. E., Kingsbury, B., and Merry, S. E. "Indicators as a technology of global governance", *Law & Society Review*, 2012, 46(1): 71–104.

Diamond, L. J. and Morlino, L. *Assessing the Quality of Democracy*. Baltimore, MD: Johns Hopkins University Press, 2005.

Dolowitz, D., and Marsh, D. "Learning from abroad the role of policy transfer in contemporary policy making", *Governance*, 2000, 13(1): 5–24.

Dourish, P. and Bell, G. *Divining a Digital Future Mess and Mythology in Ubiquitous Computing*, Cambridge, MA: MIT Press, 2011.

Engelbart, D. C. *Augmenting Human Intellect: A Conceptual Framework*, Menlo Park: Stanford Research Institute, 1963.

Fabri, M., Jean, J.-P., Langbroek, P., and Pauliat, H. eds. *L'administration de la justice en Europe et l'évaluation de sa qualité*, Paris: Montchrestien, 2005.

Frydman, B. J. *Le nouveau management de la justice et l'indépendance des juges*, Paris: Dalloz, 2011.

Grindle, M. Governance Reform: The New Analytics of Next Steps. *Governance*, 2011, 24(3): 415–418.

Haggard, S., MacIntyre, A., and Tiede, L. "The rule of law and economic development", *Annual Review of Political Science*, 2008, 11(1): 205–234.

Hammergren, L. "Expanding the rule of law: Judicial reform in Latin America", *Wash. U. Global Stud. L. Rev.*, 2005, 601.

Haas, P. M. "Introduction: Epistemic communities and international policy coordination", *International Organization*, Winter 1992, Knowledge, Power, and International Policy Coordination, 46(1): 1–35.

Jarrahi, M. H. and Sawyer, S. "Social technologies, informal knowledge practices, and the enterprise", *Journal of Organizational Computing and Electronic Commerce*, 2013, 23(1–2): 110–137.

Kerwer, D. 'Rules that Many Use: Standards and Global Regulation,' *Governance* 2005, 18 (4), 611–32.

Knill, C. *The Europeanization of National Administration*, Cambridge: Cambridge University Press, 2001.

Maple, C. "Security and privacy in the internet of things", *Journal of Cyber Policy*, 2017, 2(2): 155–184.

Merryman, J. H. *Law and Social Change in Mediterranean Europe and Latin America*. Stanford, CA: Stanford Law School, 1979.

Morlino, L. Changes for Democracy, Oxford: Oxford University Press 2011

Pech L, Scheppele K.L, 'Rule of Law Backsliding in the EU: Learning from Past and Present Fail-ures to Prevent Illiberal Regimes from Consolidating within the EU', Cambridge Yearbook of Euro-pean Legal Studies. 2017.

Piana, D. 'Unpacking Policy Transfer, Discovering Actors,' *French Politics* 3, 275–97, 2007c.

Piana, D. Retour à Glasgow: normativité, performativité et gouvernance du judiciaire en Europe, in B. Frydman e A. van Waeyeberge (eds), *Gouverner par les standard et les indicateurs*. Bruxelles, Bruylant, pp. 263–275, 2014.

Piana, D. De la qualié du droit à la qualité de la justice, in "Simplification et qualité du droit", *Conseil d'Etat, La Documentation Française*, pp. 241–246, 2016.

Radaelli, C. The Politics of Europeanization Kevin Featherstone and Claudio M. Radaelli Oxford University Press Oxford, 2003

Rose, R. *Lesson-Drawing in Public Policy*, London: Chatham House, 1993.

Sandefur, R. L. "Access to what?" *Daedalus*, 2019, 148(1).

Stone-Sweet, A. and Sandholtz, W., 'European Integration and Supranational Governance,' *Journal of European Public Policy*, 1997.

Schimmelfenning F, Sedelmeier U Governance by Conditionality: EU Rule Transfer to the Candi-date Countries of Central and Eastern Europe. J Eur Publ Policy 2004, 11:669–687.

Scott, J., Trubek, D. "Mind the gap: law and new approaches to governance in the European Union", *European Law Journal*, 2002, (8)1: 1–18.

Stone-Sweet, A. 'Judicialization and the Construction of Governance,' in M. Shapiro and A. Stone-Sweet (eds), *On Law, Politics, Judicialization*. Oxford: Oxford University Press, 2002.

Trubek, D. M. *The Rule of Law in Development Assistance: Past, Present, and Future*, "Occasional Papers", Wisconsin: University of Wisconsin, 2004.

Turner, S. "What is the problem with experts?" *Social Studies of Science*, 2001, 31(1): 123–149.

Verdonschot, J. H., Barendrecht, M., Klaming, L., Kamminga, P. "Measuring access to justice: The quality of outcomes", SSRN Electronic Journal 2008, 10.2139/ssrn.1298917.

Wittkower, D. E. "Technology and discrimination", in *Spaces for the Future: A Companion to Philosophy and Technology*, edited by J. C. Pitt and A. Shew, New York: Routledge, pp. 37–64, 2018.

Woolgar, S. "The turn to technology in social studies of science", *Science, Technology, & Human Values*, 1991, 16: 1–20.

Xia, C, and Maes, P. "The design of artifacts for augmenting intellect." In Proceedings of the 4th Augmented Human International Conference on – AH 13, 154–161. Association for Computing Machinery, 2013.

6 A new compass for legal professionals, stakeholders, and policy makers

A dance of intelligence

Right at the start of the 20th century Henri Matisse, at the request of Sergei Shchukin, an extremely entrepreneurial Russian art collector, painted the "Danse", a magnificent portrait of what we may safely define as a karmic, powerful, and prototypical ritual unveiling a foundational column of our social living: interdependence under conditions of common sources of rhythm-norms. Exhibited at the Grand Palais des Champs in the autumn of 1910 and hosted still today, upon a donation by the New York Museum of Modern Art, the "Danse" is a perfect metaphor of the compass we need to ensure that the governance of the digital transformation that takes place within the justice system complies with – and is responsive to – the social ontology of the interaction that people and justice experience.

Empirical reasons recalled in Chapters 3, 4, and 5 support the claim made in this chapter and the proposal that, accordingly, is put forth herein. Information technologies function more as enablers and catalysts than determining factors of changes; legal and judicial actors are depositaries of easily available knowledge and tacit know-how that interact with the systems designed to reorganize, render digitally, and transform the justice systems. The combination of standards that regulate both the design of the new digital infrastructures and the computational devices must respond to a people-centred vision of the demand for justice. This means that a "by design" quality embedded into the digital infrastructures is not a sufficient condition to ensure the quality of justice delivered to citizens. A couple of examples will cast sharp light on the point. The design of the dataset where judicial acts are recorded must respond to a standard of technological quality – such as security – as well as legal standards – such as anonymity. However, these standards are necessary but not sufficient conditions: readability, accessibility, and intelligibility for citizens are equally important. How do we combine these different standards, without a prior rank of priority, is the issue today on the agenda of the domestic and international institutions? A "one-size-fits-all" recipe that applies standard principles and a cultural measurement of quality will feature a low degree of responsiveness and, therefore, a low degree of legitimacy. See on quality measurement in the context of the socio-legal and political systems Diamond and Morlino (2005). In the picture sketched out in the previous chapters a pivotal stakeholder is missing: companies holding the advanced expertise and the specialized professionalism to design and develop digital infrastructures for the justice systems. Information systems' designers and artificial intelligence developers feature today an extraordinary capacity to influence the market and to hold the position of gate-keeper in the access to quality.

On top of that, over the last two decades an increasing number of law firms invested in the development of case law analytic tools, due diligence methods, and information technology platforms to interact with users and institutions. Scholars that carry out their research at the crossroads of information technology engineering and legal studies argue that the key step in the development of artificial intelligence devices consists in the selection of the sample for training, that is, the information used to create an algorithm. This selection relies on analysis of the legal and judicial texts. The participation of legal and judicial actors at this early stage looks like a necessary condition to ensure that the "intelligence" of the technological support "dances" to the same "music" followed by the justice systems. It seems that the early steps play a crucial role: developers and users must engage in a collaborative dialogue to ensure that the "augmented" justice system not only performs well – which means to be respectful of managerial standards – but is also respectful of the other non-technical standards mentioned above (Peter 2009).

In this chapter a concrete proposal is put forth. The proposal goes back to the initial two principles, humanism and pluralism, and the serious assessment of the meaning a "crisis" has. The model sketched herein is inspired by:

1) a comprehensive view of the cycle of knowledge that unfolds within the justice systems. Professionals, officers, and experts who perform their roles within the justice systems contribute not only to creating knowledge, but also to perpetuating the practical applications of that knowledge. They are also crucial in the innovation and revision of that knowledge. The model put forth in the following pages aims to value, at the highest possible level, this cycle of knowledge's creation, sharing, and transfer.

2) a participative method of system design (Barley 1986; Simonsen and Robertson 2013). This approach reminds the stream launched during the 1960s and 1970s to respond to a growing pressure emerging from the bottom to "have a say" on the design of information technology systems (Simonsen and Robertson 2013). The novelty proposed here consists in the participative method applied recursively to the development of the systems and to the process of standard setting that aims to regulate the systems. The key notion that must to be borne in mind is "recursive". The proposal values highly the recurrent and regular performance of all the steps proposed, from the participative design to the evaluation of evidence-based use, to the elaboration of standards, and to the – this is the crucial point – composition of these standards on the basis of a people-centred approach. A process of scrutiny investigating legal needs must be at the basis of the regulative matrix. A deep and empirically responsive knowledge of the way justice systems function must be, equally, at the basis of the design of the digital infrastructures.

Towards a citizen-centred standard-setting process

The critical review of the analytical grid that is, more or less explicitly, accepted as a pillar of this paradigm is inspired by the observation of the practices of digital revolution unfolded into the legal and judicial sector as well into the realm of digital forensics and by the mapping of the "information technology-driven" reforms adopted in the European member states and in the associated countries. The *pars destruens* is followed up and turned, so to say, into a positive step, by advancing to the outline of a new multi-dimensional framework, which stems from previous researches carried on in the field of the quality of justice and the quality of democracy assessment.

Moving the epistemological and methodological baseline requires a shift of the paradigm to avoid falling victim to an institutional design that is disconnected from the reality and from the actual rationales that shape the interaction between society and justice systems. Chapters 3 and 4 showed the shortcomings of the mainstreaming vision, which tends to forget both the heterogeneity of the demands of justice and the complex nature of justice, which has been described as a system of kinds of intelligence. If the heterogeneity represents an empirical reason to adhere to a strong call for a human-centred approach, the complexity of the justice system recalls the foundational role that must be acknowledged to pluralism.

Chapter 3 and 4 told a different story about the existing interaction among legal services, demands of justice, and judicial reforms inspired by the digital transformation. This story features a high degree of misfit with the mainstreaming discourse, especially when it is applied to the horizon opened up by the computational rationality applied to the law and the justice sector. This misfit is fertile terrain for paradoxes and risks of legitimacy erosion. The paradoxes deal specifically with three principled ideas that the justice institutions are expected to embed into their practices and to enforce in the way they deliver to citizens and social groups. The first paradox refers to the promise of equal treatment as an outcome of the technological reform. To outline it briefly, the main argument put forth in favour of the technology-driven reforms claims that due to the standardizing effects triggered by the software and the digital devices, litigants interacting with partly digitalized courts or digital legal services will receive a more equal and homo-genous response. This is challenged empirically by analysing the cases where formal guarantees of equal treatment are defined in the civil and criminal procedural codes and, at the same time, high degrees of territorial and organizational differential treatments coexist: Italy. The second paradox deals with the promise of an increased trust in the judi-ciary and the legal institutions as an effect of the hyper depersonaliza-tion of the proceedings. This argument is challenged by analyzing in comparative terms the trends featured by the European member states in terms of reforms and trust in the court system. The outcome of this quantitative analysis will be strengthened with an in-depth case study of the UK (England and Wales) platform of digital reform in the justice sector. As a matter of fact, the intensity of the application of digital devices in the justice sector does not correspond to the positive trend featured by trust rate. Finally, the third and, eventually, the most salient paradox is the one that connects to the promised increased autonomy and impersonality of the trials and to the pre-judicial legal treatments of disputes. This is questioned in reality by a number of cases where the applications of the AI turn into a biased and discriminatory pro-cedure. The point is highlighted in those contexts where disputes touch upon the enforcement of social rights or rights that have been violated into highly contrasted or polarized social contexts. As a matter of fact, algorithms and digital devices seem to be particularly shortcoming when they are asked to stand up to the level of the ideal promises made by their promoters.

The proposal herein developed argues on a completely different line. Two variables play a pivotal: professionalism and governance. This is a way to say that actors do matter and human intelligence is welcome in the new legal and judicial universe where artificial intelligence and digital technologies are fully exploited and incorporated not as a replacement of human reasoning, rather as an empowerment mechanism of embedded collective institutional intelligence.

Furthermore, the analysis that is offered in the following pages and the empirical evidence narrated and interpreted throughout the analytical reasoning unfolded here are both bringing about a scientific effort to respond to a global question we have queried for almost a decade: does digital technology entail a paradigmatic change in institutional and social life? Shall we qualify it as a major shift in the species of our way of functioning in the democratic setting we are familiar to? Or rather should we abandon any resistance and accept that this is a genuine change in the genus of our common living and, consequently, in the way we set up rules and norms to ensure that in social contexts our individual dignity and fundamental rights are still protected? This question, as general and abstract as it sounds, directly impinges upon the quality of citizens' daily life. The salience and the significance of the disruptive potential of digital technology shed light on how we consider the justice sector.

A fair, accessible, accountable, and equal-to-all-system of justice is one of the most desirable goods citizens wish for and one of the pivotal functions democratic institutions are expected to perform. This is the case with even more salience and timelessness in the contemporary EU, where increased mobility, countless economic and commercial transactions, and the traditional coexistence of differences are today coupled with an ever-growing range of expectations that citizens have about the quality of their individual and social lives. If justice systems are key for the quality of life of EU citizens, digital technology, including big data and artificial intelligence tools, is shaking institutionalized behavioral patterns, ways of solving collective problems (Schwab 2016), and ultimately the knowledge-action link which lies at the basis of all decisions allocating resources or values.

This is, first and foremost, the reason we have to consider digital justice and transformation technology as a potential for EU citizens and institutions, as well as a paradigmatic challenge to the traditional way rules are enforced and disputes settled. To be more concise, digital technology shakes EU practices of justice delivering and the institutional guarantees of a fair trial (Lessig 2001).[1] The introduction in the justice

---

1 It refers to the web based innovations by qualifying them as a new method of making innovation (second part). This is to say that we are not facing a quantitative change, rather we are experiencing a qualitative shift of paradigm of social living and human thinking.

systems of algorithm and IT devices, which support legal reasoning and judicial decision-making, has a disruptive potential.

And yet, despite the huge debate already provoked worldwide, the transition into judicial systems equally accessible to all citizens and equally responsive to all demands of justice remains a vast "construction site". The EU has not fallen behind the frontier marked by the new progress and launched a comprehensive strategy to reflect upon the potential big data has for the lives of citizens, institutions, and the economy.[2] Scholars are also aware of the challenges we are facing: they claim a revisit of our "epistemology" (Kitchin 2014). There is wide consensus that not only evidence-based policies are highly sensitive to this issue (Jayasuryia and Ritcheske 2015), but also (and foremost) that rule-making and rule enforcement processes, that traditionally have taken place in relation to a "context" or a territory, may be disanchored because of the global availability of information on human behaviors, habits, trends, and so on (Silbey 2011).

The focus on delivering the capacity and effectiveness of justice systems seems to have been dominant so far, arguing that decisions taken on the basis of, or thanks to powerful IT devices and digital rationales are more reliable because they stem from a bigger and more vast quantity of information (Aubert 2014). Others contest that data analysis and data mining are driven by notions and classifications (algorithms) that are bias conducive and scarcely accountable to the larger public. And yet, "digital justice" (Lassègue and Garapon 2018) questions the current approach to innovations: should we assess innovations on the basis of a purely managerial, output-oriented understanding of the quality in the public sector or, instead, should we rather evaluate the changes triggered by innovations in a more comprehensive and multidimensional manner, which calls for an innovation policy and requires broad public awareness? To translate the innovative potential in better justice systems for EU citizens, we need a more refined approach to combine law, artificial intelligence, social demands for rights, and dispute settlement.

Empirical evidence covering a vast set of practices and institutional settings should take very seriously the challenges that stem from digital revolution and hit the justice systems. This will lead to a path-breaking proposal that takes stock of the lessons drawn from previous researches and institutional experiences, which cast a new light on the interplay

2 www.europarl.europa.eu/news/en/press-room/20170209IPR61709/big-data-libe-meps-call-for-better-protection-of-fundamental-rights-and-privacy.

between "quality of the machinery" and "quality of services" delivered to citizens and merges socio-legal studies with AI and data science studies.

This proposal expands the focus and empirically addresses the following questions: 1) Which social and institutional implications originate from the digital revolution? 2) To what extent do citizens enjoy a higher level of quality of justice when justice is provided on the basis of a matrix combining information technology devices, algorithm, and natural reasoning? 3) Would citizens accept being judged by algorithms rather than by human beings if this ensures equal treatment and rapidity of judgment? 4) Which are the patterns of interaction between algorithm-driven decisions and traditional professional skills, such those of the judges, prosecutors, lawyers, police, and intelligence staff?

To frame these questions from a people-responsive perspective, one must accept the idea that digital technology is an enabler to deliver citizen-centred services in the justice sector, but also recognize that the "enabling" dimension of digital infrastructures is only part of a more complex story, where a range of potentials and phenomena need to be addressed with an evidence-based, interdisciplinary, and multi-dimensional framework.

To rise up to this epistemological and social challenge, socio-legal research must rely upon a mixed methodology, combining the analysis of a dataset covering the trends featured by national systems with the in-depth reconstruction of organizational practices and professional norms and the investigation of the citizens', businesses', and social groups' attitude towards digital justice and extra-judicial mechanisms of dispute resolution.

This will allow an evidence-based assessment of the impact of digital technology and artificial intelligence on the independence and accountability of judicial decisions; on the quality of justice delivered and experienced by citizens; on the role that legal experts, data scientists, and civil society organizations should play to ensure that digital justice complies with citizens-centred standards.

The impact assessment will be a crucial building block of a more comprehensive governance mechanism, where both the standard setting process and the stakeholders' participation are ensured on the principle that humanism and pluralism have to be interlaced into a dynamic governance process – where design, development, use, critical evaluation, and revision are tied up together into a virtuous circle.

Technologies and guarantees

The quest for better knowledge in order to inspire better decisions is not new to scholars and policy makers. Nor do the issues relate to the growth of the potential of artificial intelligence in the human and social sciences. Since the first decades of the 20th century the ideal of a stronger computational performance has joined the promise of more efficient, more effective, and therefore more readable and predictable decisions. In the 1990s, the dimensions of the complex puzzle information and governance took on a new look (Woolgar 1991). This is the reason why today several facets of the digital and computational transformative potential for social and institutional systems stand at the crossroads of three fundamental research fields.

Technological developments touching upon public institutions and business organizations have gained the highest position in the social and political agenda for decades, both from academic and practitioner perspectives (Hasselblad and Kallinikos 2000; Clarke and Newman 1997).[3] This research field is largely influenced by two different and still interlaced puzzles: the interaction between humans and objects – notably between intentionality and machinery – and the interaction between material and immaterial (Nardi and Kallinikos 2012). Two ideas have been influential in these respects: the notion of hybrid agent and the notion of socio-technology – where ICT is conceived as a sociological phenomenon. The focused nexus thereby is the convergence of social media, mobile computing, cloud-based ICT, and information stemming from the vast big data available on worldwide platforms of services, intermediations, and storage (Jarrahi and Sawyer 2013). The cost-effective computation and the abrupt decrease in costs of access to information and data have been easily and widely deemed as a powerful leverage of organizational efficiency and ideas/actions responsiveness.[4]

As a matter of fact, the rise of a new approach to public governance, pivoting on the modernizing effects engendered by the introduction of information technology tools and a performance-oriented strategy, dates back to the late 1990s and the early 2000s. In Chapter 1, the path

---

3 See the Organisation Science special issue https://pubsonline.informs.org/pb-assets/OS_special_issue_emerging_technologies_and_organizing_2019withlogos-1554151898287.pdf and the forthcoming special issue on AI and work transformation "Information System and Society" https://pubsonline.informs.org/doi/full/10.1287/isre.2018.0784.

4 *The Digital Revolution: What's on the Horizon?* www.researchgate.net/publication/260604267_The_Digital_Revolution_What%27s_on_the_Horizon [accessed 28 July 2019].

dependence that links the waves of modernizing policies experienced in the public sector to the favourable conditions encountered by the recent introduction of digital infrastructures and technological devices in the fields of justice administration – among other key policy sectors, such as health care and education – has been extensively described. The claim made here adds to that description and highlights the expectations raised through these waves of policies, namely the transformation of the public sector and the improvement of the citizens/ public institutions interaction. The improvement was expected, featuring a higher degree of transparency, accountability, and – most importantly – equal treatment.

The attraction of the ICT as a way to regain efficiency tuned into the ongoing stream of public administrative reforms already launched in the late 1980s as one of the major outcomes of the new public management. International studies have developed since then, and reframe the subject of citizens/public governance interplay in terms of efficiency, accountability, transparency, and effectiveness and add to these criteria the burden of the quality of public goods by means of which governments and local authorities satisfy the needs of citizens in vital areas: justice, health, education, utilities, infrastructures, administrative procedures for business (Katsh and Rabinovich-Einy 2010 on justice; Kruse and Beane 2017 on health; Beetham and Sharp 2007 on education; Maple 2017 on security, to refer to the most prominent works). The points raised above are differently appraised within the studies developed on the quality of democracy and the quality of government (Mungiu-Pippidi 2015).[5] In this research field, technology in general and information and data more specifically, are related to the legitimacy of the decisions taken by rulers and citizens' representatives in three respects: a) more pluralistic information and more accessible data create more favourable conditions to hold institutions and rulers accountable to citizens and stakeholders (Rothstein 2011); b) technology, and more specifically digital technology, once injected into the public institutions at the interface between citizens and governmental organizations, decreases the costs of accessing institutional spaces, and reading and understanding institutional decisions; c) technology and automation are triggering a new wave of modernization within public professionals and bureaucratic bodies; d) rather than replacing decision-making rationality and traditional expertise by automated devices, calculus, and

5 See also "Shall we need to praise for a digital democratic rule of law?", in *New York Times*, 5 August 2018.

highly specialized scientific and technological expertise, this new wave generates new patterns of interplay where old and new are interlaced .

The aspects recalled above are the fundamental reasons why the application of digital tools and computational rationalities in the justice systems rapidly gained top position in the agenda of international and transnational *fora*. This holds in the setting of the United Nations (2018) as well as within the Council of Europe, the OECD, and the European Union, without leaving behind the most influential private actors and think tanks.[6] National governments as well felt the need to investigate the interplay between people's rights, the quality of legal services, and the digital infrastructures that irrigate the organizations and the institutions that produce, deliver, and monitor the latter. This has taken the shape of expert committees such as in France,[7] or *Stiftungen* debates – such the Bertelsmann in Germany[8] and the Leonardo Foundation in Italy[9] – or technology assessment bodies as in Denmark and in the Netherlands.

Therefore, three compelling failures of the traditional governance modes praise the adoption of an "augmented intelligence" (Engelbart 1962; Xia and Maes 2013) in the public governance: a) discretionary power of public officers as a bug driving the public systems towards discrimination; b) inefficiency and ineffectiveness as a need for transparency-oriented public management; c) opacity and lack of readability of expert-based decisions which calls for automated expert systems where readability and accessibility may "simply" depend on laypeople's' digital literacy. Yet, the outcome of automation as a direct factor of openness and inclusiveness seems to be much less genuine than expected.

A responsive toolkit

As already mentioned in Chapter 2 and Chapter 5, the growth of technological applications and the widespread expectations arising from it are compelling reasons to acknowledge the potential of digital infrastructures to change the social and the institutional dimensions of our world (Shabbir and Anwer 2015) and, by that means, to trans-figure – for the better – the justice that is delivered to people.

6 www.unicri.it/in_focus/on/UNICRI_Centre_Artificial_Robotics
7 www.cnil.fr/en/algorithms-and-artificial-intelligence-cnils-report-ethical-issues
8 www.bertelsmann.com/news-and-media/news/arvato-systems-creates-artificial-intelligence-competence-cluster.jsp
9 https://fondazioneleonardo-cdm.com/en/ricerche-e-progetti/umanesimo-tecnologico-e-intelligenza-artificiale/

Yet, more efficiency, more data and information do not automatically evolve into better policies and better decisions. If the quality of decisions impinging upon citizens' lives is more than a robust mathematical method, then to make the design and the use of digital infrastructures consistent with principles of fairness, transparency, and non-discrimination becomes a vital quest for all societies and governments (Wittkower 2018; Sunstein 2017).

A widespread awareness of the critical facets of digital infrastructures emerged in the aftermath of some events that recently hit the public community and called for heightened attention to the discriminatory potential and, equally, to the uneven impact on all the intelligences embedded in the justice system. Spanning from organizational practices, tacit rituals, experts, and structures of intermediation – such as triage units, alternative dispute settlement providers, lawyers, law firms, legal consultants, legal representatives of enterprises – the massive injection of digital technologies and computational rationalities applied to legal diagnosis, legal analytics, due diligence, automated services, called for a revisit of the regulative framework and governance mechanisms that are responsible for ensuring the quality of justice for all.

In order to clarify the method outlined, two preliminary remarks must be made. One refers directly to the criticism of the discriminatory potential that has been addressed to both the digital technology and the computational applications – such as artificial intelligence. The empirical evidence at our disposal today shows that digital literacy may be a critical aspect of a society: the uneven distribution of knowledge and skills that are requested to interact with the legal and online justice providers creates an intrinsic obstacle to the achievement of equal access for all if equal access is meant to be facilitated by the digital transformation *per se*. Besides this, which refers to the organization of the interface demand/supply of legal services, a further point was raised on the basis of the empirical evidence (Jarrahi and Sawyer 2013). One of the most highlighted is the case of Compass,[10] a tool used to detect the propensity to become recidivist in the context of criminal procedural law in US, subjected to judicial review to counter-balance the potential discriminatory effect of its application (Pasquale 2019; Lacour and Piana 2019).

The burning scandals following the procedural and substantial legitimacy of electoral processes and political campaigns – such as Cambridge Analytics – created a pick of worldwide alarm and a demand for transparency and accountability in the collection, use, and reuse of big data. Easy readings of these social and institutional facts, endorsing

---

10 www.propublica.org/article/how-we-analyzed-the-compas-recidivism-algorithm.

a vision of the human/machine interaction based on the simple notion of replacement or efficiency boost, would not only be misleading but also deeply irresponsive to the reality we are living in (Hildebrandt 2016).

This is exactly the concern inspiring the call for action by the European Union on digital infrastructures and digital societies. This action is instantiated by the creation of a European High Level Experts Group (HLEG) in 2018.[11] The HLEG firmly argues that, despite the distinctive information and technology core, digital infrastructures are not exclusively a phenomenon of hard sciences and computation. They are much more. In saying this, the European Union is not alone. All international fora highlight that digital infrastructures are deeply reshaping the human-machine interaction (WEF 2019), the patterns of business and management (OECD 2019), and the way in which know-ledge is produced and transferred (UNESCO 2019). This also holds in the context of legal services and justice systems. The recent outbreak of the health and subsequent institutional emergency due to the pandemic has triggered an increasing intensive process of standard setting and monitoring to detect potential breach of the fair trial guarantees due to the sudden and unprecedented shift to the remote and on line organisa-tion of key functions of the States, such as the legal and justice services. In this context the documents resulting from the international fora assessment exercise offer an interesting view about the need to combine societal accountability to managerial efficiency. See OECD, 2020 and European Commission, 2020.

All evidences and expert discourses maintain that digital infrastructures and computation applied to the justice sector are an interdisciplinary and multi-faceted phenomenon, influencing the foundations of soci-eties: human rights, human dignity, the quality of our living together at all levels, local, national, transnational, and global. This is exactly the epistemological vision that inspires the proposed approach, which draws a line to tune governance into not only the current approach towards privacy, data protection, and cyber-security (Bennett 2018; Hoofnagle 2019), but also into a socially responsive perspective.[12]

Beyond the pluralism of stakes and visions, the aspects highlighted above create a potential synergic understanding of values and principles that must fuel *both* the design and the use.[13] In fact, justice institutions,

---

11 https://ec.europa.eu/newsroom/dae/document.cfm?doc_id=56341.

12 The European policies touching the issue of data are manifold. An important part is played by the economic understanding of data as a resource within the economic development. Balancing between privacy and economic growth has consequently become a key issue. See Cavanillas, Curry, and Wahlster 2015.

13 https://ec.europa.eu/research/participants/data/ref/h2020/grants_manual/hi/ethics/h2020_hi_ethics-data-protection_en.pdf.

legal services providers, the technology-oriented market, and stakeholders are building altogether an eco-system, one that converges on admitting that instead of being a replacement of human reasoning and acting, *technological and computational intelligence* are, rather, revealing our human nature; it forces us to revisit the notion of human intelligence and puts human beings in a completely new setting where traditional mechanisms of coordination and collective actions are comprehensively reshaped.[14]

To translate this approach into a real model of governance, an innovative scientific approach is necessary. This entails integrating decision-making processes unfolded by public service institutions; and an integrated and participatory method to make the design and the use accountable and responsive to societies' notions of fairness. The rule of law mechanism launched by the European Commission, which includes a "consultative momentum", goes in a similar direction, even though the model proposed here covers the entire cycle of the scenario, design, use, assessment, and feedback, which seems to be vital to make digital infrastructures responsive to legal, technical, and social criteria. In this vision it is possible to meet three major challenges: 1) increasing public and private engagement in the design and application accountable to both social and technical standards; 2) preparing private and public decision-makers to act on the basis of a hybridized rationality, where human and technological kinds of intelligence are combined in a readable, responsible, and explicable manner; 3) ensuring an appropriate framework to tune *legal services and justice institutions as they are transformed by the digital turn* into European values, by means of which discrimination is absolutely avoided and at the same time a plural set of norms – legal and ethical – hold designers and users accountable.[15]

The new approach relies on the studies elaborated on the quality of justice and on the scholarship that has built strong bridges between society and technologies. It will enable stakeholders, users, and policy makers to connect policy analysis to scientific investigation. It will build upon the norms and practices elaborated by practitioners and stakeholders as developers and users to revisit the notion of accountability in the public

---

14 https://ec.europa.eu/digital-single-market/en/high-level-expert-group-artificial-intelligence.

15 By framing the rule of law mechanism in the context of the broader functioning of the political system "justice system, anti-corruption framework, media pluralism, and other institutional issues related to checks and balances' (this is how the Report delivered by the European Commission reads in the Summary of the Stakeholders Consultation), the European Commission outlines a practice whose potential is close to the model sketched out in these pages.

sector. The ultimate goal is to create the scientific, the professional, and the institutional preconditions (Though recommendations) that will ensure that AI and digital technology – which is at the basis of the big data-driven automation tools trained to support decision makers – is a catalyst of trust, granted by citizens to public institutions.

International studies addressing the issues of technology and computation are making a claim about the possibility of injecting those normative principles into the design that create fairness and, thereby, legitimacy. Scholars and regulators who claim for a "design" approach are certainly making a good point, which is not sufficient though. By claiming that infrastructures gain the whole of the quality they need by means of a properly and adequately projected design, they fall victim to an epistemological fallacy, which consists in adopting a deductive and linear vision of social processes. If the digital infrastructures that enter into the justice sector are ontologically socio-technological facts – instead of being purely technics – then the design is just a first, preliminary step along the way that ensures the fairness and legitimacy of legal services as they are provided to the laypeople, either on the basis of a highly efficient digitalized organization or on the basis of a highly optimal computational device of law analytics.

The epistemological posture that justifies the "design" approach is misleading once policy makers and regulators move on and engage in the standard setting process. A missing link creates a critical hiatus between reality and regulation. This link consists of the empirical knowledge that is necessary to cast light upon the actual interplay between technologies and actors, that is, the hybridization of the kinds of intelligence that take place "in context". The way laypeople address the legal service providers they demand, their concerns, and their problems are of an empirical dimension that regulators and designers need to know. More importantly, which rank should be assigned to each of the criteria taken into consideration in the model herein proposed – legal, technical, social, managerial criteria – is more an empirical question than a "a-priori" assumption. It is more a matter of combining than a matter of excluding. Finally, the acclimatization that takes place within the courts and the law firms when they incorporate tools driven from technical and computational intelligence – ranging from devices of court management to due diligence devices and case law analysis – is an empirical dimension that deserves consideration in the context of the regulation.

The usable knowledge elaborated through empirical research and monitoring to build a pluralistic regard, that enables critical thinking and responsible engaging into the entire process of policy making, is a crucial element of the new compass proposed here. This is the scientific ground on which a new compass for better governance must set up an embryonic pilot with a regulative stance, imbued within the system of institutions which have jurisdiction over digital technology, data protection, and ethical technology. The action plan of a better compass twins this to a comprehensive set of lifelong training programs for decision-makers and the public.

The added value of this proposal is therefore threefold. It fills the gap between actual social needs of public services and soft law on a trustworthy set of digital infrastructures for the justice system; it tunes up a set of digital infrastructures for the justice system with quality standards of governance, rule of law and human development; and it elaborates a durable and transferable methodology, infusing it with an inclusive method to set the regulation of digital infrastructures.

Actors and strategies

Participative design and evidence-based policy making are not new in the spectrum of the methods of governance. As a matter of fact, at the crossroads between technology and politics is a new season of regulation inaugurated during the last two decades of the 20th century. This season is marked by the pilot experiences of new governance modes which discontinue the top-down approach and the dominance of the procedural-formal rationality. In the context of this shift, the rise of participatory methods to assess the policy impact of technological and scientific innovations traces a red line between different countries, on both sides of the Atlantic. One of the most promising experiences is represented by the model set up in Denmark which incorporates and institutionalizes the combination of three principles: public openness, technical soundness, and political accountability. Established in 1985, the Technology Assessment Board aimed to pursue a balanced combination of public awareness and political autonomy from the unavoidable influence exercised by the technology market. Reformed in 1995, the appointment mechanism adopted for the Danish Technology Board staff provides interesting insights about the multiple agency that seems to be necessary to hold highly sophisticated technologies accountable to society:

> the DBT director constitutes the link with the council, which has general responsibility organization. We will call this board Executive Board (EB). More largely, the EB is made up of 11 members (plus the director) responsible for the budget and the development of the work program. Four members are appointed by the Minister of Science and Technology (after consulting Parliament), a member by a network of citizens, a member by the Union of Public Servants,

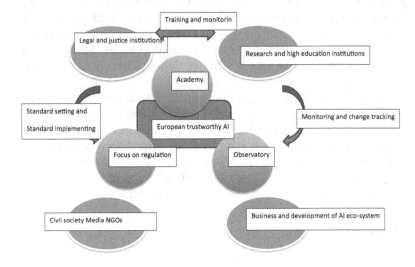

Figure 6.1 "Three Pillars-Model of governance" as it may be framed in the European context

a member by the coalition of unions, a member by the coalition of employers' organizations, a member by the Council for the Development of Danish trade, one member by counties and municipalities and one member by research councils.

(Delvenne 2006)

Despite the positive impact of the participatory method on the legitimacy of the technology assessment, a clear distinction between the stage of "listening" and the stage of the "decision" appears necessary. The evidence at our disposal today about poorly structured dialogue between society and science points to a potential failure both in consolidation and in continuity, which are both preliminary conditions needed to set up a reliable method of governance. Therefore, the functioning of the model proposed here is accordingly based on a two-step timeframe, which aligns the dialogue with the frame of political leadership, both in permanent connection with research and with the technology market. The institutional model will therefore take the shape as illustrated in Figure 6.1.

The model will pivot on the following:

1. the academic function is based on high school training courses, but also on the laboratories which supervise doctoral students, and all

the actors who have a training mission, building strong links with the practices stemming from the implementation of artificial intelligence solutions and the uses which citizens can testify.
2. the observatory function opens a dialogue to be built between the associative partners, socioeconomic and industrial perimeter, AI research teams, each field application offering research, training and sharing opportunities; and
3. the authority function turns to the knowledge built through the two previous pillars in institutions involved in the certification, validation, and regulation of AI and, more broadly, inserts the products of this knowledge into the public space.

This is to flesh out a European model of governance of the digital infrastructures applied in the justice system which combines the quality of the procedures, the fairness of the results, and the responsiveness to the practices and expertise of stakeholders. These three functions may be supervised by three functional committees:

1. the Academy Committee, focused on training, is also responsible for mapping training needs (including continuing education). It meets once a year.
2. The Observatory Committee, focused on research, monitors the results of research on practices as shared activities between academics and industry. It meets once a year.
3. The Authority Committee, focused on recommendations for regulators, has a mixed composition of academic and institutional. It meets once a year and liaises with an international forum with law and technical intermediaries.

As portrayed in Figure 6.1, the new compass aims at elaborating a ground-breaking research method, resulting in a vision of technology applied within the interplay between society and justice systems based on three components – legal, ethical, and technical – which is then mirrored into a three-sided governance model. In the context of this model, the consistency of justice systems as transformed by the digital turn with the EU hard and soft laws on fundamental rights, data protection, and privacy is in the scope of action of the Authority; the responsiveness of the technologies integrating the experts' decisions is in the scope of the Observatory's assessment; and the capacity of stakeholders and citizens is guaranteed by the Academy. This link with the research is vital to create the methodology and usable knowledge for the achievement of the applied research objectives – notably the scientific sustainability of the reforms adopted in the justice systems alongside the scientific and the technological advancements. If considered within the context of the European Union, the model feeds into the overall pattern of the European oversighting institutions, comprising the ECHR, the EDPS, the European Ombudsman, and the EAFR,[16] and puts into a long-term perspective the work done by the HLEG both on the ethical dimensions of artificial intelligence and digital economy and on responsible investments in technological development.

Open data government and reuse of data collected in the public sector have now gained the highest priority in the public sector. This is for a number of key reasons, among which three come first:

1. Data and big data feature a degree of availability, diffusion, and persistency somehow unknown in the past; the digital format provided by the dataset, notably as they are drawn from the functions of public institutions deployed alongside the territories and public organizations, allow a cross-sectional data analysis and a massive in-depth data analysis. The computational rationality applied to public actions seems to have consequently gained great momentum.
2. The idea of evidence-based policies is now highly appealing as it meets the call for a more objective action in the public sector. Citizens and enterprises ask for more intelligible and more reliable action. This fits an approach based on data and the evidence drawn from them.
3. The cognitive potential of big data is largely underexplored. This happens in several cases because in the public sector, whereas central institutions handle the dataset, at the periphery or in the local articulations – such as agencies, offices, services – chief officers and servants do not share common methods and languages to use and to reuse data.

This state of the matter is particularly significant in the justice sector where a further cultural shift is now taking place: one that shifts the justice sector from a purely rule of law sector to a justice sector that fits the broader spectrum of public governance.

The DOG project – Data – Organization – Governance – is the first integrated project launched to structure all the data available today in the justice sector in Italy, to run a meta-analysis of the data, to train chief officers on the meaning and the potential of the data, to elaborate a "tableau de bord" to manage the judicial offices and the justice

---

16 European Court for Human Rights (ECHR), European Data Protection Supervisor (EDPS), European Agency Fundamental Rights (EAFR).

administrative functions, and to frame local and central administrative actions – dealing with resources, objectives, quality standards, strategies of structural investments – in a common methodological approach allowing the central institutions to speak to the local actors speaking a common language.

The project aims at delivering three key results:

- The atlas of justice administration dataset;
- The *tableau de bord* for judicial administration organizations – both central and local;
- The set of training modules for justice administrators – general directors, administrative chief officers, as well the high-ranking officers in the related organizations.

Trustworthy legal services for all

Trust is key in social relationships and is vital in the legitimization of institutional actions. As already stressed, trust is more a dynamic equilibrium than a stock of resources that a social system may take for granted. Moreover, trust does not apply only and exclusively to the interplay between people and institutions, such as in the justice sector where people seek legal solutions to their problems and the justice system is expected to reply on the basis of a range of services that ensure fairness. Trust is meaningful for the quality of justice also within the matrix of justice institutions, at play between different actors: either within the court system or between the court and the law firms. Reliability is therefore a vital component of the well-functioning of the justice system. This applies even more to digital infrastructures that reshuffle the mechanisms by which actors coordinate. Interactions in presence are reshaped profoundly. Communications and acts of creating a shared sense are equally transformed.

By pointing to the central role that trust must play in the design of digital technologies and computational applications to the justice system, the international leaders are doing things right. However, there seems to exist a mismatch between the principled idea of trustworthiness and the actual processes by which trust is created, maintained, and eroded. The question of how trustworthiness may be created is largely unanswered.

The proposal sketched out herein aims at filling this gap by taking stock of the lessons provided by the empirical research in the socio-legal domain, in the organizational sciences, and in the political processes. The most compelling outcome of the researches conducted on the interaction between actors and rules consists in questioning its genuine linearity. This holds also in the field of behavior that takes place in a context regulated by standards. Standards do not determine the behavior of organizations and actors. In contemporary times, most of the time actors are obliged to abide by several standards, which provide a different and not necessarily coherent normative framework. When justice institutions and legal services providers meet technology and computation, they are forced to bridge between legal norms, technical standards, and managerial criteria. The resulting complex is the empirical object that must be focused on and targeted by regulative actions. Overlooking the coexistence of these normative foci will mean downplaying the role that regulation and accountability must play in promoting better justice for all under the conditions set by the digital revolution.

The proposal takes full benefit from the variety of scholarly streams developed in the field of quality of governance and soft law, as well as in the domain of new public management and accountability, and innovates in the following fundamental respects: 1) the interplay between agency and rules; 2) a pluralistic vision of normativity; 3) a multi-dimensional notion of accountability; 4) the notion of trustworthiness.

Therefore, the added value has to be assessed after considering the aspects mentioned above.

At the micro level, the proposal endorses a vision that directly focuses on the context where actors are situated and operate. This new compass distances itself from the notion of hybrid agent and works on a notion of "multiple agency" which refers to the recurrent and recursive interaction between actors and *technologies*. This is to deal directly with the "human computation problem" (Von Ahn and Dabbish 2008) and values the proposal put forth to speak of "augmented intelligence" in cases of complex decision-making processes where human and artificial rationales are combined. AI is accordingly defined as a set of rules that impinges upon the architecture of choice (Sunstein 2017) and thereby deeply and permanently influences the context where actors interact.

Unlike the approaches focusing on the relationship between one rationale of decision and one norm, the proposal tracks the work done across the comprehensive and worldwide standing research agenda on justice systems, and supports a multiple notion of normativity. Norms and standards by which the combination of kinds of intelligence, individual as well as embedded into organizations and institutions (such as rituals) in the production and delivering of public services, must be assessed are legal, ethical, and technical. This rich notion is used to focus the dynamics of change and adaptation unfolding at the level of situated actors – businessmen, designers, client supporters, policy makers, legal experts, court chief justices, and mediators.

This reasoning leads to developing a comprehensive understanding of the legal services delivered through digitalized, or partially digitalized, and automated, or partly automated, infrastructure. Trust is herein considered an ongoing process linking up citizens to policies and goods. Accordingly, trustworthiness is not the linear outcome of the augmented intelligence compliance applied to the public service with a single standard; moreover, trustworthiness results from a combination of different norms and standards according to which technologies must be assessed legally, ethically, and technically. The degree and the relative proportion of the three within the combination depend on the culture of the society where public services are enjoyed.

References

Aubert, B. "Providing an Architecture Framework for CyberJustice". *Laws*, 2014: 721–743.

Barley, S. "Technology as an Occasion for Structuring". *Administrative Science Quarterly*, 1986: 78–108.

Beetham, H. and Sharp, R. *Rethinking Pedagogy for a Digital Age*, London, Routledge, 2007.

Bennett, C. Regulating Privacy, New York: Cornell University, 2018.

Cavanillas, J. M., Curry, E., and Wahlster, W. *New Horizons for a Data-Driven Economy: A Roadmap for Usage and Exploitation of Big Data in Europe*, New York: Springer, 2015.

Clarke, J. and Newman, J. *The Managerial State*. London: Sage, 1997.

Delvenne, P. and Brunet, S. "Le Technology Assessment en question: Une Analyse Comparative Pierre Delvenne et Sébastien Brunet CRISP". *Courrier hebdomadaire du CRISP*, 2006: 5–63.

Engelbart, D. Augmenting Human Intellect, Report, available at https://www.dougengelbart.org/content/view/138, 1962.

European Commission, Rule of Law Report, Brussels, Official Publications, 2020.

Hasselblad, H. and Kallinikos, J. "The process of rationalization: A critique and re-appraisal of neo-institutionalism in organization studies", *Organization Studies*, 2000, 21(4): 697–720.

Hildebrandt, H. *Smart Technologies and the End(s) of Law*, Cheltenham, UK: Elgar, 2016.

Hoofnagle, C.J., Designing for consent. Journal of European Consumer and Market Law 7(4): 162–171, 2018.

Jayasuryia, K. and Ritcheske, K. *Big Data, Big Challenges in Evidence-based Policy Making*, Minnesota: West Academic Publishing, 2015.

Jarrahi, M. and Sawyer, S. (2013), "Social technologies, informal knowledge practices, and the enterprise," *Journal of Organizational Computing and Electronic Commerce*, 23(1), doi: (14) (PDF) Social Technologies, Informal

Knowledge Practices, and the Enterprise. Available from: www.researchgate. net/publication/263075568_Social_Technologies_Informal_Knowledge_ Practices_and_the_Enterprise [accessed Nov 16 2020

Katsh, E. and Rabinovich-Einy O. *Digital Justice: Technology and the Internet of Disputes*, Oxford: Oxford University Press, 2010.

Kitchin, B. "Big Data, New Epistemologies and Paradigm Shift". *Big Data and Society*, 2014: 1–12.

Kruse, C. and Beane, A. "Health information technology continues to show positive effect on medical outcomes: Systematic review", *Journal of Medical Internet Research*, 2017, 20(2): e41.

Lacour, S. and Piana, D. "Faites entrer les algorithmes! Regards critiques sur les scénarii de la justice prédictive", *Cités*, 2019, 80(4): 66–88.

Lassègue, J. and Garapon, A. *Justice digitale*. Paris: PUF, 2018.

Lessig, L. *The Future of Ideas*, London: Random House, 2001.

Maple, C. "Security and privacy in the internet of things", *Journal of Cyber Policy,* 2017, 2(2): 155–184.

Mungiu-Pippidi, A. *The Quest for Good Governance: How Societies Develop Control of Corruption*, Cambridge: Cambridge University Press, 2015.

Nardi, B. A. and Kallinikos, J. eds. *Leonardi*, Oxford: Oxford University Press, 2012.

OECD, *Recommendation of the Council on Artificial Intelligence*, OECD/ LEGAL/0449, 2019.

OECD Policy Brief. Access to Justice and the Covid 19 Pandemic, Paris, Official Publications, 2020.

Pasquale, F. "A rule of persons, not machines: The limits of legal automation", *George Washington Law Review*, 2019, 1: 8.

Peter, A. Koechlin, L., Förster, T., Zinkernagel, G. F. *Non State Actors as Standard Setters.* Cambridge: Cambridge University Press, 2009.

Rothstein, B. *The Quality of Government: Corruption, Social Trust, and Inequality in International Perspective*, Chicago: University of Chicago Press, 2011.

Schwab, K. *The Fourth Revolution.* Geneva: World Economic Forum, 2016.

Shabbir, J. and Anwer, T. "Artificial intelligence and its role in near future", *Journal of Latex Class Files*, 2015, 14(8): 1–11.

Silbey, S. "Legal Culture and Cultures of Legality". In *Handbook of Cultural Sociology*, edited by J. Hall, 470–479. London: Routledge, 2011.

Simonsen, J. and Robertson, T. *Routledge International Handbook of Participative Design.* London: Routledge, 2013.

Sunstein, C. R. *Republic: Divided Democracy in the Age of Social Media*, Princeton: Princeton University Press, 2017.

UNESCO *Principles for AI: Towards a Humanistic Approach?*, Paris, Official Publications Office, 2019.

Von Ahn and Dabbish Designing games with a purpose Communications of the ACM, 51(8):58–6, 2008.

WEF, Data Collaboration for the Common Good Enabling Trust and Innovation Through Public-Private Partnerships, 2019, www3.weforum.org/ docs/WEF_Data_Collaboration_for_the_Common_Good.pdf

Wittkower, D. E. "Technology and discrimination", in *Spaces for the Future: A Companion to Philosophy and Technology*, edited by J. C. Pitt and A. Shew, New York: Routledge, pp. 37–64, 2018.

Conclusion

A choral perspective

In the masterpiece *Machines Like Me* (2019), Ian McEwan provokes all of us with a critical question:

> Autonomous has never been the appropriate adjective, provided that the new machines depend as new born on massive networks of computers connected to satellites and radars. If the artificial intelligence must lead to a safe way back home, which set of values and priorities must be set up within the digital device?

Who is left with the responsibility of choosing the values and the priorities? More importantly, which criterion is left with the rationale of setting the quantum of each value and the metric on the basis of which the priorities are ranked? This is the same question raised in Chapter 3, just worded differently: for laypeople to trust justice systems we need to go beyond a monistic view of the quality of justice, such as the one that is adopted by either centring on the legal normativity or on the managerial normativity the burden of the quality of justice.[1] To go beyond the epistemological monism, we need to endorse a comprehensive view of justice systems, that is, systems comprising many dimensions and responding to several different criteria of quality, such as the social criterion and the professional criterion. A context where justice is delivered by a perfectly-in-time mechanism of delivering, despite being efficient, may fall short of the demand for justice, if this demand consists in the

---

1 In the book we have repeatedly claimed that an exclusively procedure-focused view of quality or an exclusively efficiency-focused view of quality fall short in accounting for the comprehensive notion of quality that is suitable to understand the quality requested by citizens and social groups. This is the point raised about the limits of a monistic approach to quality.

recognition of the stance and the grievances of the claimants. A context where justice is delivered by a mechanism where the role for the human dimension is ample and the empathy is valued beyond the performance may fall short of the demand for justice, if this demand consists in the request of a fast, timely, and clear response to an economic dispute. More generally, the sense the claimants and laypeople in general give to their demands must be one of the criteria among the other criteria that are taken into account to assess the quality of justice. This statement holds with even more urgency and salience regarding the justice systems that integrate digital devices and applications of artificial intelligence. If I know that the judge's reasoning is based on several components – such as substantial legal categories applied to the specific case, scientific or technical evidence that is deem salient to adjudicate the case, evidence taken through witnesses' hearing, and so on – that are compounded and elaborated through a legal framework, I need to know that I can trust the reasoning method, the legal framework, the professionalism of the judge, and the array of mechanisms that lie at the basis of the production of these "hints". If these arrays of elements incorporate computational and technological kinds of intelligence – in the sense we have referred to Chapter 4 – I need to be assured that the experts that have the responsibility for developing the technological and computational kinds of intelligence are held accountable. This must happen not only with regard to technical accountability. It must also happen with regard to public and professional accountability. In a nutshell, as Chapter 6 has strongly argued, the governance of the digital infrastructures that enter into the field of the legal services, the court management, the legal and judicial reasons, the legal and judicial drafting, and in the channels of communication between actors of the justice systems, must be based on a multiple agency, where public and private actors, technical experts and legal experts, and stakeholders of the organized civil societies engage in a structured and institutionalized ·dialogue. Mutual scrutiny and mutual accountability are key leverages of quality: the quality that comes from this model is more a dynamic process than an *acquis* that can be taken for granted.

To build on this argument, the book has built upon the evidence presented in Chapter 3 and Chapter 4. Along the same lines sketched in the first chapter, the digital transformation is a human affair. It takes place within the justice systems through complex patterns of interdependence, whose rationale calls for a multi-dimensional and a pluralistic approach. This approach is both epistemological and institutional. The proposal sketched out in the book stems from the empirical evidence social sciences have been developing for several decades, by focusing on the pathways followed to reform justice systems – in some contexts with a comprehensive package of innovations, in other contexts with a more punctual and tailored set of measures. The evidence put at the disposal of legal experts, decision-makers, and stakeholders points to three aspects: 1) the path-dependence effects originated from the subsequent waves of reforms that impinged on the functioning of justice systems; 2) the differential rationale of the demand of justice, which stems from the differential needs laypeople experience in their daily lives; 3) the coexistence of different kinds of intelligence, which, altogether, interact within and through the justice systems and, by that means, represent the relevant humus that the research and the policy makers must consider in the context of the digital infrastructure design.

An uneven and differential distribution of key aspects offers strong reasons to step back from a monistic approach in the design of the model by means of which a society governs the digital infrastructures that are integrated within justice systems. The word "monistic" echoes the choice of a dominant discipline to inspire this design as well as the choice of a dominant player to master the *mise en oeuvre* of the design, once this latter has been adopted.

As stated in the first chapter, only time will tell if the method adopted is the more effective and efficient. The outcomes that emerge are visible and measurable in due time. And yet, the emphasis of this book is on the urgent need for a "multiple-voice", pluralistic, and societally accountable model of governance. This entails revisiting and reorganizing three aspects: 1) the policies targeting the competences and the professionalisms that are at play within the justice systems; 2) the mechanisms by means of which the normative standards that are at play within a justice system that integrates digital infrastructures – legal, technical, mathematical, organizational – are compounded into an overall framework that outlines the ranks and the measures of the quality delivered to laypeople by justice systems; 3) the balance to be ensured between societal accountability and technical accountability, in order to avoid falling victim to a technocratic and reductionist approach – unable to speak truth to society.

A role to play for the "knowledge-holders"

What this book is about, in short, is a proposal for a multi-agency and inter-disciplinary regulative mechanism, which incorporates a recursive cycle of digital and technological tools' design, development, use, assessment, and critical review, running under conditions of transparency and public answerability. For a long time, regulation was expected to be the most suitable response, although, in some circumstances, the difficulty encountered first in fabricating the regulation and then implementing it convinced us to shift the focus of regulatory expectations on soft law, for example on standards and guidelines, or white papers. But, in any case, without embarking on the venture destined to sink the applicative differences and the consequent dumping not only of the market, but also, and above all social, of regulating everything with the legally binding formalization. Alongside this first impasse there is another one, which concerns "who makes the rules" and above all "who undertakes to ensure that these are respected". And it is here that the game between governments and companies, especially large companies which are actually characterized by a complex and institutionalized corporate governance, becomes strategic.

In truth, we have been told that it is up to governments to make the rules, but the real truth, the one that is also on the side of scientific research, is that the rules are partly built by those who have the expertise to build the devices that must be regulated and which already integrate forms of self-regulation into their architecture. It is even good that this is the case. In the world of computer engineering, physics, aerospace engineering and bioengineering, to give just a few exhaustive examples of the immense universe that technological innovation has opened in recent years, the rules are already partly within the engineering processes of innovations with a high density of epistemic capital. The exceptionally high specialization acts as a barrier to the very possibility of making everything governable in a heteronomous way.

We should capitalize on past experiences and make them a compass for the government of what is in effect a tool for the production and distribution of a public service, that is, that set of services that will be provided, guaranteed, explained, made accessible – or more properly that they must be guaranteed to be made accessible and intelligible, that is, worthy of trust and reliability – to the citizens, with a truly integrated and standardized network equipment. We do not want to deal here with the question of the profiles, although existing, of competition and competitiveness. Instead, we want to share what we have learned from past experiences and research. Neither law nor regulation alone can be sufficient. To ensure that infrastructural investments are oriented towards the creation of a public good which in turn has a very strong impact on the guarantee of access rights to services, it is necessary that all actors carrying knowledge and observers of strategic practical knowledge are involved. Comparative empirical evidence shows this not only by looking at the different European countries, but also at the different sectors of public policy.

We need a compass that takes into account not only the moment of technological design, but also research and empirical knowledge of the use of technology, which somehow "nourishes" governance with the knowledge that is born – in the literal sense of the term because we are talking about discovery – from the encounter between a designed technology and its use in the context in which this happens (Woolgar 1991; Jarrahi and Sawyer, 2013). Therefore, in public governance there must also be a moment that periodically integrates the monitoring of what happens when the network and the services that travel towards the citizen meet citizens and businesses, from these "return" – in the form of experiential data analysed in a structured and methodologically rigorous way – to the actors who have regulatory powers. Digital infrastructures and ICT devices applied to the justice systems require a fully fledged "public governance" (Dourish and Bell 2011), in the sense of conceived for the res publica, and participated along the whole chain of knowledge construction from the technical to the organizational, economic, and social by the actors who are not just stakeholders, but also knowledge-holders. This makes public governance good governance for a trustworthy public space.

In short, digital technologies and artificial intelligence are too serious potentials for disruption and transfiguration, when they penetrate the justice system. We must ensure that the overall outcomes of the legal, managerial, computational, professional, technological, and social kinds of intelligence are continuously interacting, under the same rhythm. It will look like *a chorus that "speaks trust" to power*.

Index

Note: Page numbers in *italics* refer to figures. Page numbers followed by 'n' and a number refer to notes e.g. 50n1.

Abbott, K. 90
accessibility 27, 49, 69, 102, 118; cost reductions 4, 12, 19, 21, 22, 26, 77, 100, 101; *see also* equality of access
acclimatization mechanism 79–80, 84, 87, 106
accountability 44, 99, 101, 103, 116; *see also* governance; managerial accountability; public accountability
ADAJ project (Accès au Droit et à la Justice/Accessing Law and Justice) 65
ADR (Alternative Dispute Resolution) 26, 29, 31–32, 103
agency: change driver 28; human agency 4–6, 53, 62, 94, 99; hybridized agents 79, 100, 105–106, 112; multiple agencies 15, 25, 76, 82–83, 94–95, 99, 105–107, 112, 116; theory of 72; *see also* human/artificial dichotomy; pluralism
Agenda 2030 10, 42
AI *see* artificial intelligence (AI)
algorithms 9, 12, 13–14, 32–34, 96, 98–99; *see also* datasets
Alternative Dispute Resolution (ADR) 26, 29, 31–32, 103
Angelou, Maya 71
arbitrariness, perception of 29, 39, 52, 53, 56
Argyris, C. 66

Aristotle 73
artificial intelligence (AI) 11, 29–34, 40, 68; governance 80–82, 94, 99, 105, 108, 112, 115, 119; *see also* algorithms; human/artificial dichotomy

bar associations *18*, 19, 23, 82
Barocas, S. 33
Belgium 25, 31–32, 41
Belloubet, Nicole 26
Berger, P.L. 56
Bomberg, E. 88
Botero, J. 72

Calvino, I. 57
Cambridge Analytics 103
Campbell, T.A. 30
Canada 64–65
Caplan, Joel 13
case law analytics 5, 12, 22–24, 30–33, 69, 94, 106
case management 19–20, *21*, 22, 25, 27, 32
Centre de Justice de Proximité du Grand Montréal (CJPGM) 64–65
CEPEJ (European Commission for the Efficiency of Justice) 14n5, 20–21, 30, 74–75, 80–81
change *see* crisis, definition; digital transformation; disruption caused by technology; theories of change

chief justices 23, 24, 25, 26, 68, 85, 113
citizen-centred framework 2–3,
  12–13, 28, 39, 41, 53–54, 93,
  95–99
Commaille, J. 3, 4, 35, 45, 72
Commission Européenne pour
  l'Evaluation de l'Efficience des
  Systèmes Judiciaires (CEPEJ)
  14n5, 20–21, 30, 74–75, 80–81
communication 26–27, 62, 64–65, 74,
  79, 111, 116
COMPAS software (Correctional
  Offender Management Profiling
  for Alternative Sanctions) 13,
  33–34, 103
compass of governance *see* three
  pillars (compass) model of
  governance
computational rationalities 4, 11, 40,
  68, 81, 96, 102, 103, 110; *see also*
  algorithms; datasets
context: cultural context 35, 40,
  45–47, 49–54, *55*, 78, 79, 113;
  definition 49; globalization 98;
  national differences 41, 43, 77–81,
  89, 96; organizations 68, 85–88;
  social 47, 49–50, 53, 54, *55*, 56, 80,
  97; three pillars (compass) model
  52–53, 93, 106–107, 112, 119
cost reductions: access to justice 4,
  12, 19, 21–22, 26, 77, 100, 101;
  learning costs 77, 85, 87
Council of Europe 20–21, 30, 43, 58,
  74, 102
court system *18*, 32, 34, 45, 53–54;
  court management 19–21, 24,
  26–27, 58, 74, 77, 116
crisis, definition 1–2, 94
cultural context 35, 40, 45–47, 49–54,
  55, 79, 113; a-cultural indicators 78

Danse (painting) 93
data analytics 11–14, 27, 84, 98, 110,
  119; case law analytics 5, 12, 22–24,
  30–33, 69, 94, 106
Data – Organization – Governance
  (DOG) project, Italy 110
datasets 11–14, 40, 93, 97–100, 103,
  106, 110; case laws 12, 22–24,
  30–33, 69, 94

Davis, K.E. 67, 78
De Monticelli, Roberta 5
decision making *see* judicial
  decisions; policy design
Delvenne, P. 108
demand-offer justice cycle 18, *18*
demands of justice 55; heterogeneity
  of 44, 48, 73, 95, 117; impact of
  technology 31–32, 34; overload
  19, 32, 43, 75, 78, 98; response to/
  satisfaction of 29, 42, 48, 54,
  58–59, 81–82, 115
dematerialization 7, 20, 23–25, 28,
  83, 100
Denmark 41, 102, 107
digital infrastructures, definition 6
digital transformation 50, 80–81,
  97–99, 105, 109, 113, 116; three
  waves 22–27
digitalization 10, 11, 20, 23–25, 32, 83
discrimination 12, 18, 33, 80, 96, 98,
  102–103, 105
dispute resolution 13, 26–32, 41, 47,
  53, 69, 75, 97, 103
disruption caused by technology 7,
  14, 18, 26, 31, 40, 50, 97, 119
document management 19–20, 21, 22,
  25, 27, 32
DOG (Data – Organization –
  Governance) project, Italy 110
Dolowitz, D.P. 89
Douglas, M. 50, 66

economic crisis 2007–2008 19, 21
economic development 28–30, 42, 44,
  51, 54, 59, 72
effectiveness: governance 41, 77, 84;
  impact of technology 13, 28, 67,
  75, 98, 100–102
efficiency: governance 63–64, 67,
  74–75, 78, 100–104, 106, 115;
  impact of technology 9–10, 19,
  21–22, 27–29, 31–33, 43, 52
enforcement mechanisms 7, 9,
  44–45, 49–50, 53, 78, 118; rights
  enforcement 42, 58–59, 73,
  75–76, 96–98
England and Wales 25, 96
epistemology 11–12, 35, 44, 72, 95,
  98–99, 104–106, 115–117

equality before the law 7, 34, 54, 72–73
equality of access 26, 34, 54–55, 59, 63–65, 72–73, 83, 96–98, 103
European Commission 58
European Commission for the Efficiency of Justice (CEPEJ) 14n5, 20–21, 30, 74–75, 80–81
European Convention of Human Rights 23, 74–75
European Ethical Charter on the use of artificial intelligence in the judicial systems and their environment 14n5, 30, 80–81
European High Level Experts Group (HLEG) 104, 109
European Justice Scoreboard 27
European Social Survey 40–41
European Union: and digital technology 83, 97, 102, 104; governance 59, 74, 77, 83, 85–86, 88–91, 105, 109; and justice systems 59, 77; member states' divergence 41, 83
Europeanization process 88–91, 105
Ewick, P. 2–3
experts, role of 13–14, 83–90, 94, 99, 101–102, 109, 116

fair trial 12, 14, 23, 34, 58–59, 74–75, 77, 97
fairness 34, 40–41, 43, 47, 51, 63, 72; governance 83, 97, 103, 105–106, 109, 111
France 11n4, 23, 26–27, 31–32, 41, 64, 102

Garapon, A. 32
Germany 64, 102
Godson, R. 51
governance 6, 8, 43, 58, 75, 88, 101–102; *see also* participative design of governance; standards-based governance; three pillars (compass) model of governance

Hardin, Russell 47
HLEG (European High Level Experts Group) 104, 110

human/artificial dichotomy 12–13, 34–35, 53, 60, 96–97, 99, 104–105, 112; judicial decisions 13, 23–24, 32–33, 35, 69, 98–99, 102
humanism 4–6, 53, 62, 94, 99
hybridized rationality/agency 79, 100, 105–106, 112

impartiality 34, 41, 44, 45, 47, 59, 73, 75
intelligence(s) 68–69, 102–106, 112, 116–117, 119; definition 10–12, 59–62; embedded into justice system 32, 60–61, 69, 96–97, 103; *see also* artificial intelligence (AI)
intelligibility of justice system 28, 34, 49, 55–56, 60–62, 93–94, 110, 118; *see also* readability of justice system
Italy 23, 31–32, 41, 79–80, 96, 102, 110

Jessop, Bob 88
judges 19, 21, 23–24, 40–41, 51, 58, 68, 116
judicial decisions: human/artificial dichotomy 13, 23–24, 32–33, 35, 69, 98–99, 102; quality indicators 23–24, 27, 32–33, 44, 62–63, 78, 80
judicial function 19, 44
judicial independence 11n4, 41, 43, 44, 58
judicial institutions, overload 19, 32, 43, 75, 78, 98
justice, definition 40, 48, 51
justice system, definition/components 3–4, 18, *18*, 22, 51, 53–54

Kant, I. 45, 49
Katsh, E. 26
Kingsbury, B. 67, 78
Knill, C. 77
Koselleck, Reinhart 1

La Porte, Caroline de 88
Lassègue, J. 32
learning costs 77, 85, 87
legal needs 2, 3n3, 36, 42, 54, 64n1, 83, 95

legal norms 5, 55, 78, 88, 112–113, 115
legal services 36, 43–44, 49, 52–55, 61, 73, 82–83; uses of technology 22, 24, 29, 31, 111–113
legality 39–43, 47
legitimacy: of ADR 26; governance of policy 79, 85, 89, 94, 96, 105–107; of justice system 36, 51, 53, 59, 63, 101; of rule of law 46–47
litigation, rates of 29, 46, 59, 75
Luckman, T. 56

machine learning 11–12, 32–34, 69, 81, 83
Machines Like Me (novel) 115
Mahler, Gustav 61
managerial accountability 58, 65–68, 98, 112, 115
Manners, I. 88
Marsh, D. 89
Matisse, Henri 93
McEwan, Ian 115
Merry, S.E. 67, 78
Mulgan, Geoff 10
multiple agency engagement 15, 25, 76, 82–83, 94–95, 99, 105–107, 112, 116

Netherlands 13, 23–25, 31–32, 41, 102
normativity 4–5; and context 47–49, 52, 79; European norms 73–74, 77, 88, 89–90; and intelligence 5, 10, 112; legal norms 5, 55, 62, 84, 88, 105, 111, 115; pluralism 5, 112–113, 115; and policy transfer 84, 87; social norms 4, 5, 29, 49
Norvig, P. 30

OECD (Organisation for Economic Co-operation and Development) 8, 50n2, 77, 102; Agenda 2030 10, 42
Online Dispute Resolution (ODR) 13, 26–27, 29, 30

participative design of governance: examples of 90, 107; multiple agencies 15, 25, 82–83, 94–95, 99,
105, 106, 112, 116; recursivity 76, 82–83, 95, 99, 105, 112, 117, 119; *see also* pluralism; three pillars (compass) model of governance
people-centred perspective *see* citizen-centred framework
Peterson, J. 88
Pinzon-Rondon, A.M. 72
pluralism 1, 5, 35–36, 94–95, 99, 106, 112–113, 115–117
policy design 35–36, 45, 49, 75–76, 79, 88, 98–99, 104–107, 110
policy implementation 24–25, 77, 79–80, 84–88, 99, 104, *108*
policy transfer method 84–85, 87–90, 99
Pratt, C. 72
public accountability 26, 35, 58, 78, 83, 105, 112, 116, 117

qualitative analysis 12, 73
quality of justice: definition 2; impact of technology 27–28, 33; methods of evaluation 58–59, 65, 99, 105, 111, 115–117; need for evaluation 41–43, 58–59, 63, 73–78, 80, 86–87, 93, 103
quality of life 39, 72, 97, 104
quantitative measuring 28–29, 66–67, 72, 77–78, 81, 84, 96, 106

Rabinovich-Einy, O. 26
readability of justice system 14, 62, 64, 93–94, 102, 105; *see also* intelligibility of justice system
recursivity 76, 82–83, 95, 99, 105, 112, 117, 119
regulation *18*, 19, 29, 80, 95, 106–109, 112, 117–118
reliability 10, 32, 48–49, 75, 77, 98, 111, 118
rights enforcement 42, 58–59, 73, 75–76, 96–98
rule of law 39–41, 43–47, 50–51, 57–59, 76, 77, 90, 110; and equality 7, 34, 54, 59, 72–73
Russell, S. 29–30

Selbst, A.D. 33
Silbey, S.S. 2–3, 47

silence 29, 38, 49, 57, 61, 81
small claims 17, 27, 31–32
Snidal, D. 90
social context 47, 49–50, 52, 54, *55*,
    56, 80, 97
social contract 50–53
social norms 4, 5, 29, 49
socio-legal perspective 2–5, 39–47,
    50, *55*, 61, 75, 99
socio-technological phenomena 4, 5,
    100, 106
sociology of law 44–45, 63,
    66
soft laws 29, 74, 76, 79, 107, 109,
    112, 118
Sotomayor, Sonia 62
Spain 31–32, 41, 64
standardization 20n1, 23–24, 31, 35,
    43, 63, 67, 96
standards-based governance 29, 67,
    76–85, 93–95, 112–113, 117–119;
    acclimatization mechanism 79–80,
    84, 87, 106; recursivity 76, 82–83,
    95, 99, 105, 112, 117, 119
Stiftungen 102
Susskind, Richard 31

technical standards 5, 80, 83, 105,
    112–113, 116–117
theories of change 14, 35, 72,
    75–76, 80, 82; *see also* digital
    transformation
theory of agency *see* agency
three pillars (compass) model of
    governance: impetus for 1, 12,
    27–28; importance of context
    52–53, 93, 106, 112, 119; model

82–83, 95, 106, 108–109, *108*, 112,
    118–119
Tilly, Charles 45
timeframe of legal/justice process 49,
    59, 73, 74, 75, 77, 87
transformation *see* crisis, definition;
    digital transformation; theories
    of change
transparency: governance 83, 101–103,
    117; justice system 12, 41, 44, 59,
    62, 77–78; technological change
    28, 32, 67
trust: definition 44, 45, 47, 56; in
    justice system 12, 28, 47, 48–50,
    52–53, 55–56, 61, 115; national
    differences 41, 43, 96; in policy/
    governance 45, 49, 80, 83, 105–106,
    108, 111–113, 116, 118–119; in
    technology 9, 83, 105
Trust and Rules (Tilly) 45
twinning model 83, 85–86

United Kingdom (UK) 13, 25,
    32n10, 96
United Nations Interregional Crime
    and Justice Research Institute
    (UNICRI) 30, 102
United States of America (USA):
    COMPAS 13, 33–34, 103;
    USAID 58

Valery, P. 10

Wales *see* England and Wales
Weber, Max 65–66
World Bank 43, 57–58, 77
World Justice Project 2019 42

Printed in the United States
by Baker & Taylor Publisher Services